POOR MAN'S COOKBOOK

POOR MAN'S
COOKBOOK

BY GEORGE COOK

Designed by Carolyn Weary Brandt
Edited by Katherine A. Neale and Ross A. Howell, Jr.

Printed in the United States of America
Published by Howell Press, Inc., 1147 River Road, Suite 2,
Charlottesville, Virginia 22901.
Telephone (804) 977-4006.
First printing.

HOWELL PRESS

Library of Congress Cataloging-in-Publication Data

Cook, George, 1920-
    Poor man's cookbook / George Cook.
    p. cm.
    Includes index.
    ISBN 0-943231-95-7

    1. Low budget cookery. 2. Marketing (home economics) I. Title.

TX651.C66 1995   641.5'52
                                        QBI94-21340

CONTENTS

"Just use your

imagination—and

your leftovers!"

PREFACE

You can go out and buy 1,000 cookbooks but none of them will ever cook for you—you have to do the cooking yourself and if you don't already know how to cook, you'll have to learn by trial and error.

Cookbooks only offer some guidelines to go by. Who hasn't tried to cook something that looked wonderful in a cookbook but didn't end up so tasty? Those recipes are the error part of learning to cook. Trying to make new things—and failing—is how you learn.

If you were to take a poll of a group of people who were all asked to taste a given dish, you would get all sorts of responses: "It needs a little more salt," "Too sweet," "Too sour." Everyone prepares food a little differently. Your taste may not be exactly like mine. If you eat food cooked by someone else, don't expect it to taste just like yours. So, when someone doesn't like your cooking, don't take it personally. Perhaps you wouldn't like theirs, either.

To be a great cook, you have to experiment—try new things and hope they turn out well and never let yourself fall into a cooking rut. If a cookbook recipe calls for a certain seasoning you don't have, try to think of something you do have that you could use instead.

My wife came home one day and I had cooked a big pot of turnips. While I was cooking, I saw an apple that had been in the fruit bowl that looked like it was going to go bad if someone didn't eat it soon. So, I peeled and sliced the apple and put it in the pot with the turnips. When my wife came home she wanted to know what I had done to the turnips. "These are the best turnips I have ever eaten," she said.

Just use your imagination—and your leftovers!

Here's wishing you the best and may your cooking be the greatest.

7

SHOPPING AND COOKING HINTS

This is the perfect how-to cookbook for the beginner, the professional who's trying to stretch a buck to feed his or her family, and everyone in between. I will teach you how to make the most of your food dollar by showing you how to get up to 100 servings from a 20-pound ham, how to get the last bit of ketchup out of the bottle, and how to make the most of your leftovers, and much, much more.

The simple recipes in this cookbook are inexpensive and require little effort. You won't need a cabinet full of expensive seasonings to make these recipes. Other than the classic standbys—salt, pepper, sugar, lemon juice, vinegar, ketchup, and sweet pickle relish—you'll only need five seasonings for main dishes (garlic salt or powder, Worcestershire sauce, chili powder, sage, and soy sauce) and three other seasonings for desserts (cinnamon, vanilla, and nutmeg).

By no means am I discouraging you from improvising and adding other ingredients; I just want to stress that you do not have to use a lot of fancy seasonings and spices to make a tasty meal.

When I was growing up, most people were taught to cook by their parents. Many of them never owned a cookbook, or if they did, they rarely used it. Somewhere along the way parents abandoned the practice of teaching their kids how to cook, and as a result, many of today's young adults have limited cooking skills. Their lack of knowledge has led them to become wasteful. Because they know only a few recipes, they think cooking is boring and expensive.

The way we cook has not changed that much in the last 100 years. Modern appliances have replaced wood stoves and brick ovens. And, of course, today much of the work is done for us (which means that our food costs more than it used to). Vegetables are grown, harvested, washed, and packaged. Livestock is raised and slaughtered and the meats are processed, wrapped, and ready to cook. Meals that would have taken our ancestors an entire day to make can now be made in minutes.

Naturally, I believe my mother was the best cook in the world. I can still see her standing in front of our old shiny wood stove. Although she used a very limited number of seasonings, her cooking could stand up to some of today's best chefs'. She was also a master at stretching our food dollar. With ten kids, she had to be. That's what this book is all about—how to make a wholesome, tasty meal on a shoestring budget.

My research for this book included a survey of other cookbooks on the market. I asked my friends to tell me what they thought about some of today's most popular

POOR MAN'S COOKING HINTS

❖   To get the last bit of ketchup out of the bottle, hold it under hot running water for 30 seconds.

❖   Looking for a better way to peel an egg? While the egg is still hot, crack the egg lightly and hold it under cold running water while you peel it.

❖   If you add bread crumbs to scrambled egg batter, the eggs are tastier and fluffier and your recipe will yield more servings.

❖   Add a little vinegar or a tablespoon of salt to boiling water to help prevent eggs from cracking while you're boiling them.

❖   To prevent hard-boiled eggs from crumbling when you slice them, use a wet knife.

❖   Add $1/2$ cup of milk to the water when cooking cauliflower so the vegetable will retain its white color.

❖   Although you should never store whole tomatoes in the refrigerator, you can wrap part of a leftover tomato in plastic wrap and refrigerate it for another time.

❖   When you are cooking fish or cabbage, put a small amount of vinegar in a pan and place it near the pot you're cooking in to help eliminate odors.

❖   Use lemon juice to rid your hands of fish and onion odors.

❖   You can weld a cracked dish back together by boiling it in milk for 30-40 minutes.

❖   To keep sweet potatoes from turning dark, soak them in salted water as soon as you peel them.

❖   Never pour salt into food directly from its

cookbooks. "You'll have to go out and buy a closet full of seasonings to make these recipes," one friend commented. "They're too complex, I don't use them," another friend said.

Comments like these prompted me to write this book. With advice on everything from buying bulk goods to thawing and cleaning foods safely, POOR MAN'S COOKBOOK may become the most important cookbook you own!

WHAT YOU SHOULD KNOW ABOUT YOUR STOVE

No two stoves perform alike. Altitude, fuel type, and the stove's insulation and age all affect your stove's efficiency. For example, a new stove may cook food in much less time. So, it may

container. This method wastes salt and can ruin your food. Pour the amount you need into the palm of your hand, and then add it to your food.

❖ To spoon shortening or margarine from its container cleanly, heat the spoon with hot water or over the burner first.

❖ When cooking macaroni or spaghetti, add a little oil (vegetable oil and olive oil work best) to keep the noodles from sticking together.

❖ Lettuce will keep better if you do not wash it before refrigeration. Wash lettuce as you use it.

❖ Never cut food on your countertop; you will destroy the surface. Use a cutting board. In fact, you should have two cutting boards: one for raw meats, which can contaminate other foods, and one for everything else. You can even use a small piece of wood as a cutting board. Be sure to scrub any cutting surface thoroughly after each use to keep bacteria from growing.

❖ Ripe tomatoes are soft and red. Just because a tomato is red doesn't mean it will taste good.

❖ Never store bananas in the refrigerator. If you have bananas that are going bad, you can use them to make banana bread or peel and freeze them. Frozen bananas make a great treat for kids.

❖ If you are doing a lot of peeling, wear a Band-Aid™ around your thumb to prevent injury.

❖ Use an old washcloth, undershirt, or any other type of rag around the kitchen instead of throwing money away on disposable paper towels. If you use an old piece of cloth as a wipe-up rag, you can throw it in with the rest of your laundry and use it over and over.

❖ To get your serving plates warm before a meal, set them on top of the stove while you're cooking food in the oven.

take some experimenting to determine how your oven compares with the one used to test the recipes in this book. You may want to test your oven with an inexpensive oven thermometer, so you can adjust the temperature accordingly.

Have you ever wondered why you have to preheat your oven? Try to cook biscuits without preheating. Since heat rises, when you first turn the oven on, the top of the oven is hotter, so your food will be cooked from the top down. Your biscuits may be brown on top, but the bottom will be raw. In other words, if you don't preheat your oven, it will cook unevenly.

Your stove must be level in order to cook foods properly. Most stoves have leveling screws to correct this problem. If your stove is not equipped with leveling screws, you can use shims or some sort of wood wedges. Use a level to make sure that the job has been done correctly. If you do not have a level, place a frying pan with a little water in the middle of the oven rack. Adjust the screws, shims, or wedges until the water is distributed evenly on the bottom of the pan.

Cooking-related accidents top the list for causes of home fires. Many homemakers will leave the house to visit a neighbor or run to the corner store, leaving a burning stove unattended. This is a big no-no. If you have to leave the house, turn the stove off.

KITCHEN PEST HINTS

❖ To keep flies out of the kitchen, set a bucket of molasses in the living room.

❖ To get rid of roaches, starve them to death by keeping your kitchen clean. If you decide to use a roach spray or powder, be sure to keep it out of the reach of children and house pets.

❖ To keep ants out of the kitchen, crumble a cookie outside of the house near the kitchen wall. When the ants come out—and they will—do a rain dance on the little pests.

11

❖ To catch a kitchen mouse, bait a trap with peanut butter or cheese. You can also burn a piece of raw bacon with a match for a second or two. A mouse can't resist the smell of bacon. As soon as the lights go out, the little sucker will be running for your trap.

❖ To keep flour beetles out of your dry food, unwrap a couple of sticks of chewing gum and put them in the cabinets. I don't know how it works, but it does. Maybe the flour beetles eat the gum and die of constipation.

EQUIPPING YOUR KITCHEN

Having a big pile of pots and pans doesn't make you a better cook. When I was growing up, most kitchens were only equipped with two or three black iron frying pans, two or three boiling pots, two or three tin bread pans, several tin pie pans, and a cake pan.

Today, most kitchens are so cluttered with cooking utensils that it is hard to find the one you are looking for. My advice is to buy only what you need so you don't overstuff your cabinets. If your kitchen is cluttered, you're less likely to want to cook, and eating out is a sure-fire way to blow your budget.

"To keep flies out of the kitchen, set a bucket of molasses in the living room."

The only kitchen utensils you really need are the following:

One potato masher	One set of tongs
One set of measuring spoons	One large collander (strainer)
One set of measuring cups	One meat thermometer
One Pyrex ™ liquid measuring cup	One small frying pan
One grater	One large frying pan
One ladle	Three pots of assorted sizes with lids
One large wooden spoon	Two or three baking dishes
One large fork	One roasting pan
One rolling pin	One bread pan
One whisk	Toothpicks

Electric gadgets are nice, but they're expensive, and many of them are unnecessary. There are really only a few that you need. I would suggest an electric toaster, an electric frying pan, and a hand-held electric mixer. An electric coffee maker is also nice to have. Remember, our ancestors got along very well without any electric appliances.

KITCHEN KNIVES

Professional chefs use several different kinds of knives; they are the tools of the trade. However, as your family's chef you don't need a lot of kitchen knives. The two knives you must have are a good butcher knife and a small paring knife.

Working with a dull knife only makes your job harder. Knives are sharpened with a steel, ceramic bones, or a whetstone. If a knife is extremely dull, you will probably need a whetstone, which can be purchased at most hardware stores.

❖ If you are right-handed, hold the whetstone in your left hand. (Hold it in your right hand if you are left-handed.)

❖ Use your other hand to drag the knife along the whetstone, pushing the blade away from your body. Make sure the knife edge is touching the stone. Repeat this stroke until the knife is sharp, then turn the knife over and repeat on the other side.

❖ Never use your finger to test if a knife is sharp. The best way to tell if the knife is sharp is to hold the knife so that the cutting edge is facing you. If you cannot see the cutting edge, the knife is sharp.

KEEP KNIVES AND OTHER SHARP OBJECTS OUT OF THE REACH OF CHILDREN!

AVOID WASTING FOOD

American households probably dump enough good leftovers into their garbage cans to feed all of Russia. Today's young adults saw their parents do this and have learned from this bad example. With modern refrigeration, some leftover food can be kept for weeks. Some foods, such as homemade soups, taste even better after a day or so in storage.

Before you begin to make a meal, take a look in the refrigerator to see if you can use any of your leftovers in whatever you are making. For example, if you have some leftover corn, peas, and butter beans, you can mix them together to make succotash.

One of my friends told me that his wife never throws away any leftovers. "That is, not right away," he explained. "She puts them in the refrigerator and lets them turn green, then she throws them away."

We're probably all guilty of saying, "I'll freeze this for later, it's too good to throw away," and then forgetting about the leftovers until they're so freezer-burned they have to be thrown away. Label frozen foods with the date they were put in the freezer and cook the oldest leftovers first. Always be sure to check your freezer before grocery shopping so you don't waste money buying things you already have.

SHOPPING TIPS

Did you know . . . a pound of instant rice costs four times as much as a pound of regular dry rice?

. . . brand-name products cost a lot more than generic products, which are often manufactured by the same company?

. . . you can buy about five pounds of flour for less than the price of two pie crusts?

. . . one loaf of bread weighs about one pound and costs as much as 10 pounds of flour?

. . . for the price of two cans of biscuits, you can buy five pounds of flour?

. . . food is packaged by weight, not volume? There may be from one to four inches of unfilled space in containers and boxes. Who pays for this? We do. Think of all the trees wasted to make an oversized box. Don't be fooled by oversized packaging that can make you think you're getting more for your money than you are.

"Think about starting a back-yard garden."

When you are grocery shopping, try to stay away from the highly advertised products that are often priced higher to cover their promotion campaigns. Excessive advertising doesn't add anything to the taste of food.

Can you save by clipping coupons? You can, but in most cases coupons are offered for higher-priced brands—that is, those with huge advertising budgets. Look around for the same item in a brand that is not advertised as much and compare prices.

Don't let your kids grocery shop for you. They will buy what the TV tells them to buy, which is usually the highly advertised and higher-priced foods.

And never go grocery shopping on an empty stomach. If you're hungry, you'll probably buy too much.

Take advantage of sales. Grocery stores often price items at cost and sometimes even at below cost. If it doesn't cost too much in gas, it may be worth shopping around to pick up sale items from several stores.

Shopping at warehouses and price clubs can save you money if you are buying for a large family. But, beware of buying food in very large quantities—you may get tired of the same old thing and some of that food will go to waste.

It makes sense to buy some sale items, such as canned goods, in quantity. Canned goods can be stored for a long time, but buying frozen items in bulk can lead to waste, since people tend to forget what's in the freezer and leave things there until they are ruined.

Do not shop in a rush. Always look at the bottom shelves for the best buys. Quite often, grocery stores stock the higher-priced items at eye-level. If you are looking for something that is on sale and can't find it, ask a store employee. There may be more in the stock room.

Think about starting a backyard garden. Two tomato plants, two green pepper plants, one hill of cucumbers, and one hill of squash will yield enough vegetables for an average family. Plus, you can grow all this food in a space about half the size of an average kitchen.

FEEDING SMALL CHILDREN

Kids will say some pretty funny things about food.

When my son was a little fellow, he shoved a cup of coffee across the table to me and said, "Take the heat out of it, Dad."

My little grandchild gave her dad a banana and said, "Unwrap it, Dad." And another one said to his mom, "When you plant the garden, will you plant some hamburgers?"

Kids are finicky. If you want them to eat good, wholesome food at meal times, keep cookies and junk food out of the house. If your kids are climbing the walls like squirrels, you may want to ask your doctor about the sweets the kids are eating.

Never force your kids to eat. If you ask your doctor, he or she will probably tell you that they have never heard of a child starving to death when food is available.

A WORD ABOUT COOKING OILS

Cooking oils are made from vegetables, grains, seeds, and nuts. Different oils are better for different types of cooking. For instance, peanut oil is my favorite oil for frying chicken. Some oils have lower saturated fat contents, but it's fine to substitute a cooking oil that's cheaper than the one your recipe calls for. Remember, all cooking oils are quite fattening, so use them sparingly.

"That's what this book is all about—how to make a wholesome, tasty meal on a shoe-string budget."

BREAD

BREAD

The trial-and-error method is the best way to learn how to make homemade bread. Just try again and again until you get it right.

In the 1930s, flour and sugar bags were made of cotton cloth. There were two or three different patterns of cloth used to make flour bags. The poor used flour sacks to make clothes—usually undergarments—since it was embarrassing to be seen in a flour sack. When kids saw a classmate wearing a flour sack, they'd say, "Don't think you're cute and sweet just because you're wearing that flour sack dress and those sugar sack drawers."

My dad used to buy 100-pound sacks of flour. He'd dump the flour into a huge barrel we kept in the middle of the kitchen. I remember being awed by watching my mother make bread. She didn't use any cooking utensils—not even a bowl. She'd pile the flour on a big bread board. She'd make a cavity in the center of the flour pile and then she'd measure out the baking soda and lard in the palm of her hand and dump it into the cavity. Then she'd pour in the milk, straight from the bottle. She never spilled a speck of flour or a drop of milk on the floor.

She used her old wood stove to bake the bread. Of course the wood stove didn't have a temperature gauge or timer. My mother used her nose as her timer. She could tell when the bread was ready just by inhaling its wonderful aroma.

I was raised on homemade bread made with pork lard. Today, pork lard has been replaced by vegetable shortening. Pork lard used to be sold in five-gallon containers, but is now commonly sold by the pound. Some old-timers still use pork lard to make bread and it still works well.

When you are shopping at a bakery, you can buy day-old bread and pastries for half-price. Even though the bakery considers these goods second-rate, you can't really tell the difference in taste. If you don't see any day-old bread on display, ask the baker if there is any in the back.

BISCUITS

Making homemade biscuits does not require much equipment. You will need a mixing bowl, a rolling pin, a breadboard, and a biscuit cutter of some sort. You can even cut the suckers in squares with a knife, or use a tin can for a cutter. A glass jar can be used as a rolling pin. No store-bought biscuit can compare with biscuits made from scratch.

Biscuit dough refrigerates well. So you can make fresh biscuits for dinner and use the leftover dough to make piping-hot biscuits for breakfast the next morning.

ROLLED BISCUITS   Makes 2 dozen

Ingredients

4 cups all-purpose flour
1 Tbsp baking powder
1 tsp baking soda
1 Tbsp sugar
1 1/2 cups vegetable
     shortening or margarine
1 1/2 cups buttermilk or milk

❖ Preheat oven to 400°F.

❖ Grease cookie sheet or bread pan.

❖ Pour flour, baking powder, baking soda, and sugar into a large bowl and mix well.

❖ Add vegetable shortening a little at a time, mixing thoroughly.

❖ Use your hand or a spoon to create a well, or pocket, in the center of this mixture and pour the milk into the well a little at a time, while stirring.

❖ Using a fork or your fingers, mix the dough until all of the flour is thoroughly mixed in the batter. If the dough is sticky, sprinkle whatever touches it with flour.

❖ Remove the dough from the bowl and knead it by hand until it looks like canned biscuit dough.

❖ Roll the dough out on a lightly floured surface (a bread board or a countertop covered with waxed paper is fine) until it is 3/4-inch thick.

❖ Use a biscuit cutter, a tin can, or a knife to cut the biscuits.

❖ Place biscuits on cookie sheet and cook for about 15 minutes. When they are done, the biscuits should be golden brown.

DROP BISCUITS
Makes 2 dozen

This is another popular method for making biscuits. It requires much less work and you won't have to touch the dough.

❖ Preheat oven to 400°F.

❖ Grease a cookie sheet or bread pan.

❖ Combine everything but the buttermilk in a large bowl and mix well.

❖ Add buttermilk to this mixture, stirring well until all the ingredients are thoroughly mixed.

❖ Spoon biscuit-sized balls of dough onto the cookie sheet or into the bread pan.

❖ Cook for about 15 minutes or until they are golden brown.

These biscuits will look a little lumpy, but they taste just as good as rolled biscuits.

Ingredients

4 cups all-purpose flour

1 Tbsp baking powder

1 tsp baking soda

1 Tbsp sugar

1 1/2 cups vegetable shortening pork lard

1 cup buttermilk or milk

POOR MAN'S SWEET BREAD
Serves 4

❖ Preheat oven to 400°F.

❖ Grease a bread pan.

❖ In a large mixing bowl, beat the eggs using a whisk or an electric mixer.

❖ Add all the other ingredients—except the milk—to the eggs.

❖ Add milk and mix well. If the dough is too thick, add more milk. Mix until you have a smooth, runny mixture.

❖ Pour mixture into bread pan. The batter should be about 1/2-inch deep.

Ingredients

2 eggs

1/2 cup vegetable shortening c margarine

2 cups sugar

1 tsp soda

2 tsp vanilla

1 tsp salt

2 cups all-purpose flour

1 cup milk

22

❖ Bake for 20-30 minutes. To tell if the sweet bread is done, stick a toothpick or fork into the center of the bread. If the toothpick comes out clean, the sweet bread is done.

❖ Use a knife to cut sweet bread into 2-inch squares.

Serving suggestion: Sweet bread is good served hot or cold.

DOWN-HOME   Serves 4-6
CORNBREAD

Ingredients

2 cups cornmeal

1 tsp sugar

1 Tbsp baking powder

1 tsp baking soda

1 tsp salt

2 eggs, beaten

2 cups buttermilk or milk

4 Tbsp bacon drippings or
   margarine

Cornbread has been a staple in the South since Jamestown was settled. Cornbread is even easier to make than biscuits, since you simply pour the batter into a bread pan or a large iron frying pan. If you want more texture and flavor, you can crumble fried bacon into the batter to make crackling cornbread.

❖ Preheat oven to 400°F.

❖ Grease a large baking pan.

❖ Mix dry ingredients in a large bowl. Add remaining ingredients and mix thoroughly.

❖ Pour batter into pan.

❖ Bake for about 20-25 minutes, or until the bread is brown on top. You can also use the toothpick method to test for doneness. Stick a toothpick (or fork) into the center of the cornbread. If the toothpick comes out clean, the cornbread is done.

❖ Cut into squares and serve.

CORNMEAL SPOON BREAD

Serves 4-6

❖ Preheat oven to 350°F.

❖ Grease a baking pan or dish.

❖ Mix dry ingredients in a large bowl. Add remaining ingredients and mix thoroughly.

❖ Pour batter into pan or dish. The batter should be about 4 inches deep.

❖ Cook for about 30 minutes. When done, spoon bread looks more like pudding than bread.

Serving suggestion: Serve with a lot of butter or jam.

Ingredients

2 cups cornmeal

1 Tbsp sugar

1 tsp salt

2 tsp baking powder

2 cups buttermilk or milk

3 Tbsp margarine, melted, or
   bacon drippings

2 eggs

SALADS

SALADS

S alads are made by mixing up a mess of things in the hopes that it will be a tasty combination. You can make a large salad and keep it in the refrigerator for a quick, healthy snack. Vegetable, tuna, or meat salads can be refrigerated for three or four days in a covered container. However, tomatoes do not keep well, so you may want to wait to add tomatoes until you are ready to serve the salad.

Do not refrigerate green salads with dressing on them. Only put dressing on the salad you will eat right away, because lettuce with dressing does not keep well. You can, however, save leftover dressing and store it separately; dressing will keep well in the refrigerator for a week or so.

HOMEMADE   Serves 12
SALAD DRESSING

Ingredients

1 cup mayonnaise
4 Tbsp ketchup
1 Tbsp vinegar
1 Tbsp sugar
pinch of garlic salt or garlic
    powder
salt and pepper to taste

I have never liked store-bought salad dressings. I always thought they had embalming fluid mixed in those suckers—they will keep forever! Homemade salad dressings taste better and they'll save you a bunch of money!

Combine ingredients in a covered container (such as an old mayonnaise jar) and shake well. You can use that same container to store the leftover dressing.

POTATO SALAD   Serves 6-8

Potato salad keeps well in the refrigerator, so you can make enough for several meals. Tomatoes are expensive when they're not in season and potato salad is good without them, so if they're not in your budget, don't put them in the salad! Be careful not to use too much vinegar unless your family likes sour salads.

❖ Put potatoes in a large pot and cover them with water.

❖ Bring water to a boil and cook for about 20 minutes or until tender. Be careful not to overcook the potatoes—they should be firm.

❖ Drain potatoes and run cold water over them for 1-2 minutes. This will make potatoes firm and keep them from crumbling in the salad.

❖ Combine remaining ingredients in a mixing bowl.

❖ Add potatoes and stir gently until potatoes are evenly covered with this mixture.

Ingredients

4 cups potatoes, chopped
$1/2$ cup onions, chopped
$1/2$ cup celery, chopped
2 hard-boiled eggs, chopped
$1/4$ cup sweet pickles, chopped
1 Tbsp sugar
1 Tbsp vinegar
$1/2$ cup mayonnaise
1 Tbsp mustard
1 tomato, chopped
salt and pepper to taste

CUCUMBER SALAD   Serves 4-6

❖ Peel and slice cucumbers.

❖ Combine mayonnaise, vinegar, sugar, garlic powder, salt, and pepper in a small bowl and mix well.

❖ Pour this mixture over the cucumbers.

❖ Stir cucumbers to make sure they are covered evenly.

Ingredients

4 cucumbers
$1/2$ cup mayonnaise
1 Tbsp vinegar
1 Tbsp sugar
pinch of garlic powder
salt and pepper to taste

COLESLAW   Serves 6-8

❖ Combine ingredients—except cabbage and mayonnaise—in a small bowl and mix well.

❖ Add mayonnaise to this mixture, stirring until it is creamy.

❖ Add salt and pepper to taste.

❖ Pour this mixture over the cabbage and stir until cabbage is evenly coated.

Ingredients

2 lbs cabbage, shredded
  or grated
$1/2$ cup celery, finely chopped
1 carrot, shredded
$1/2$ cup onion, finely chopped
2 Tbsp vinegar
2 Tbsp sugar
$1/2$ cup mayonnaise
salt and pepper to taste

CHICKEN SALAD   Serves 4-6

You can use a whole chicken or chicken parts to make chicken salad. If you are cooking for a large family, it would be wise to use a whole chicken. Save the broth, bones, and scraps for a pot of soup. Tuna, ham, pork, shrimp, or just about any other kind of meat can be substituted for the chicken.

Ingredients

2 cups cooked chicken,
chopped
$1/4$ cup celery, chopped
$1/4$ cup onion, chopped
1 Tbsp sweet pickle relish
$1/4$ cup mayonnaise
1 Tbsp lemon juice
salt and pepper to taste

❖ Boil a whole chicken or chicken parts until done. (Stick the chicken with a fork. If the juice comes out clear, the meat is done.)

❖ Remove chicken from pot and allow it to cool.

❖ When the chicken is cool, chop it into bite-size pieces.

❖ Combine the chicken with other ingredients in a large bowl and mix well.

TUNA SALAD   Serves 4

❖ Drain tuna.

❖ Combine ingredients in a large bowl and mix well.

❖ If the mixture is not creamy enough, add more mayonnaise.

Ingredients

1 6^1/$_2$ oz can chunky white tuna
2 hard-boiled eggs, chopped
^{1}/$_4$ cup celery, finely chopped
^{1}/$_4$ cup onion, finely chopped
4 Tbsp mayonnaise
1 Tbsp sweet pickle relish
salt and pepper to taste

EGG SALAD   Serves 4-5

❖ Combine all ingredients—except eggs—in a large bowl and mix well.

❖ Add eggs, stirring gently to prevent the eggs from crumbling.

Ingredients

4 hard-boiled eggs, chopped
^{1}/$_4$ cup onion, finely chopped
^{1}/$_4$ cup celery, finely chopped
^{1}/$_4$ cup sweet pickle relish
^{1}/$_4$ cup mayonnaise
salt and pepper to taste

APPLE SALAD   Serves 6-8

❖ Peel and chop apples into bite-size pieces and put them in a large mixing bowl.

❖ Combine raisins, mayonnaise, vinegar, sugar, and salt in a bowl and mix well.

❖ Pour this mixture into a bowl with apples and mix well.

Ingredients

4 large apples, chopped
^{1}/$_4$ cup raisins
^{1}/$_4$ cup mayonnaise
2 Tbsp vinegar
1 Tbsp sugar
salt to taste

CARROT SALAD   Serves 4-6

❖ Use a grater to shred the carrots thinly.

❖ Combine mayonnaise, raisins, vinegar, sugar, and salt in a bowl and mix well.

❖ Pour this mixture over shredded carrots and mix well.

Ingredients

4 large carrots, peeled

$1/4$ cup mayonnaise

$1/4$ cup raisins

1 Tbsp vinegar

sugar and salt to taste

VEGETABLES

VEGETABLES

Vegetables can be boiled, fried, baked, stir-fried, or stewed. In the South, where I was raised, they boil vegetables until they are soft and tender. That's the way I like them. Boiling vegetables is simple:

❖ Use a large pot.

❖ Fill the pot with enough water to cover the vegetables.

❖ Place the pot on a burner over high heat.

❖ When the water reaches a rolling boil, add the vegetables. The water will eventually return to a boil.

❖ Cook the vegetables at a low boil until they are soft and tender.

When I was growing up, we used fatback pork to season vegetables. It tastes great, but now fatback pork costs almost as much as ham and not that many people like to eat fatback pork. So, you might as well buy a piece of pork you like, such as ham hocks, ham slices, or pork shoulder. Have the butcher slice the meat so that it can be frozen and used as needed.

Pork bacon can also be used as a seasoning for vegetables. Fry it until it is crisp and then dump the bacon and drippings into the pot with the vegetables. Use about three strips of bacon per pound of vegetables. This is especially good with beans or cabbage.

BOILED CABBAGE   Serves 4-6

Southern cooks will boil cabbage down almost to a mush. This is the way I like it.

❖ Cut the cabbage head into quarters.

❖ Fill a large pot with 2 inches of water and bring to a boil.

Ingredients

1 medium cabbage head

2 Tbsp margarine, cooking c
   or bacon drippings

1 Tbsp sugar

32

❖ When water comes to a rolling boil, add the cabbage, margarine, and sugar.

❖ Reduce heat and cook at a slow boil. If you like crisp cabbage, boil it for about 5 minutes. If you like it soft, boil it for 1 hour.

Serving suggestion: Some folks like to season their cabbage with a few drops of vinegar. Others like butter and red pepper.

FRIED CABBAGE   Serves 4-6

❖ Cut cabbage head into 1-inch squares.

❖ Combine cabbage, margarine, and sugar in large frying pan.

❖ Fry uncovered over low heat for about 3 minutes, stirring occasionally.

❖ Cover pan with lid and fry over low heat until tender, stirring occasionally to keep the cabbage from scorching.

Ingredients

1 medium cabbage head
2 Tbsp margarine or cooking oil
1 Tbsp sugar

GREENS OR SALADS

Some greens you cook. Some you eat raw. There are several kinds of greens you can always find at your grocery store. There are even two species that grow wild: watercress and poke salad. When I was growing up, you would often see people with baskets hooked over their arms searching the fields and river banks for watercress. Early in the spring, poke salad pops up all around the farms in Virginia.

But you don't see that many people looking for wild greens any more. I guess we've gotten lazy. It's much easier to go to the grocery store and pick them up than it is to gather them in the fields.

Other popular types of greens are spinach, kale, turnip tops, and mustard greens.

COOKING GREENS   Serves 4

Cooking greens is a lot like cooking cabbage.

❖ Boil about an inch of water in a large pot
with a lid.
❖ When the water comes to a full boil, add
greens and other ingredients and cover with a
lid.
❖ Boil for about 20 minutes.
Serving suggestion: Some folks like to season
their greens with a touch of vinegar.

Ingredients

2 lbs greens
$1/4$ lb pork, 3 Tbsp pork
    drippings, 4-6 slices fried
    bacon and drippings, or
    4 Tbsp margarine
1 Tbsp sugar
salt and pepper to taste

GREEN BEANS (OR "SNAPS")   Serves 6

❖ Combine ingredients in a large pot.
❖ Cover contents with water and cook at a
low boil until about $2/3$ of the water evaporates.
❖ When $2/3$ of the water has evaporated, cover
the pot with a lid and simmer for about 90
minutes.
❖ When beans are done they will be very tender.
Serving suggestion: Some folks will add butter,
ketchup, or chopped onions to their snaps.

Ingredients

3 lbs green beans
$1/2$ lb pork fat or margarine
1 tsp sugar
salt and pepper to taste

FRIED GREEN BEANS   Serves 4

Leftover cooked green beans can be fried for a
different taste.

❖ Combine ingredients in a large frying pan.
❖ Fry uncovered over a low flame for 5-10
minutes, stirring occasionally.

Ingredients

1 lb green beans
3 Tbsp margarine
1 small onion, chopped
1 Tbsp sugar
salt and pepper to taste

TURNIPS   Serves 4

❖ Peel turnips and slice them into ¼-inch
thick pieces.
❖ Add turnips to boiling water.
❖ Boil them until tender.
❖ Remove from heat and drain.
❖ While turnips are still hot, add margarine,
sugar, salt, and pepper. Mix well.

Ingredients

2 lbs turnips
4 Tbsp margarine
1 Tbsp sugar
salt and pepper to taste

SQUASH   Serves 4

❖ Cut the squash into ¼-inch thick slices.
❖ Combine ingredients in a large, uncovered
frying pan and cook over low heat for 10
minutes, stirring occasionally.
❖ Cover with lid. Cook over a low flame
until they are tender. When most of the water
has evaporated, they are ready to eat.

Ingredients

2 lbs yellow squash
1 cup onion, chopped
4 Tbsp bacon drippings or
    margarine
1 Tbsp sugar
salt and pepper to taste
½ cup water

BEETS   Serves 4-6

Beets are one of the easiest vegetables to cook.

❖ Wash beets and cut off the green leaves. Do
not cut off the roots. Place beets in a large pot
and cover them with water.
❖ Boil beets for 35-40 minutes or until tender.
❖ Drain beets in a colander and run cold water over them. The cold water
makes the beets easier to peel.
❖ Peel and slice beets and season them with salt, pepper, and butter to taste.
Serving suggestion: Some folks like to season beets with sweetened vinegar.

POTATOES

There are several different kinds of potatoes. There are Irish
potatoes, red potatoes, and baking potatoes. When potatoes are fresh out of
the garden they are called new. Most people peel potatoes instead of
washing them. If you are going to leave the skins on, make sure you wash
the potatoes thoroughly.

I like fried potatoes cooked with onions. These are not hash
browns. Hash brown potatoes are usually fried after they have been boiled.

FRIED POTATOES   Serves 6

Ingredients

2 lbs potatoes, peeled and
    sliced
1 large onion, sliced
$^1/_2$ cup water
salt and pepper to taste

❖ Cover the bottom of a large frying pan with
vegetable oil.
❖ Put potatoes and onions in pan.
❖ Fry over medium flame, stirring occasion-
ally, until the edges of the potatoes turn brown.
❖ Add water and stir well.

- ❖ Cover pan with lid and steam cook until tender.
- ❖ Salt and pepper to taste.

POTATO SOUP   Serves 4

If you find yourself with some potatoes that are getting a little old and weathered, don't throw them out. These are the pefect potatoes for a pot of soup. Making potato soup is easy and it refrigerates well, so you can cook a large pot of soup and keep it for a week.

- ❖ Peel and dice the potatoes.
- ❖ Combine potatoes with other ingredients—except milk and seasonings—in a large pot and cover them with water.
- ❖ Season with salt, pepper, and garlic.
- ❖ Boil for about 30 minutes or until celery is tender.
- ❖ Add milk. If milk does not cover contents, add more until it does. Stir well.
- ❖ Cover contents and cook until soup comes to a full boil.

Serving suggestion: Serve with crackers or bread.

Ingredients

2 lbs potatoes
1 large onion, chopped
1 cup carrots, chopped
1 cup celery, chopped
3 Tbsp margarine
1 cup milk
garlic powder to taste
salt and pepper to taste

MASHED POTATOES   Serves 6-10

- ❖ Place potatoes in a large pot and cover them with water.
- ❖ Put lid on pot and boil potatoes for about 20 minutes or until tender.
- ❖ Drain potatoes and put them in a large mixing bowl.

Ingredients

4-5 lbs potatoes, peeled and
   diced
1/4 cup butter or margarine
1/4 cup milk
salt and pepper to taste

37

- ❖ Add milk, butter, salt, and pepper, and mash potatoes by hand or using an electric mixer.
- ❖ Continue mixing potatoes until no lumps remain.

LEFTOVER MASHED POTATO PATTIES

Serves 4

Ingredients

1 lb mashed potatoes
3 Tbsp flour
1 egg, beaten
1 medium onion, chopped
2 Tbsp margarine or cooking

Leftover mashed potatoes are often thrown away. There are two ways you can use these leftovers instead of wasting them. Mashed potatoes reheat well in the microwave. In fact, they taste better reheated in a microwave than they do when warmed on top of your stove.
You can also use them to make leftover mashed potato patties.

- ❖ In a mixing bowl, combine the flour, egg, and onion with leftover mashed potatoes, mixing well.
- ❖ Use your hands to make patties out of this mixture.
- ❖ Cover the bottom of a frying pan with cooking oil or margarine and heat the oil for a few minutes before adding patties.
- ❖ Fry patties over low flame. When the undersides of the patties are brown, flip them over and cook until the other sides are brown.

BOILED SWEET POTATOES

Serves 4-6

Ingredients

4-6 medium sweet potatoes
butter or margarine to taste
salt and pepper to taste

- ❖ Peel, wash, and quarter potatoes.
- ❖ Place potatoes in large pot and cover with water.
- ❖ Boil until tender.
- ❖ Drain off water.

❖ Add butter or margarine while potatoes are still hot.

❖ Salt and pepper to taste.

BAKED SWEET POTATOES   Serves 4-6

❖ Preheat oven to 375°F.

❖ Wash the sweet potatoes and place them in a bread pan. If any of them are especially large, cut them in half so that they will all be done at the same time.

❖ Rub a little cooking oil over the potatoes and stick them with a fork in several places.

❖ Cook sweet potatoes for about an hour. When they are done, you should be able to stick a fork into them easily.

❖ Butter potatoes and sprinkle them with salt and pepper to taste while they are still hot.

FRIED SWEET POTATOES   Serves 4-6

❖ Peel, wash, and cut potatoes into 1/4-inch thick slices.

❖ Cover the bottom of a frying pan with cooking oil.

❖ Stir-fry potatoes for about 5 minutes.

❖ Add water and cover pan.

❖ Cook potatoes until tender, stirring occasionally.

❖ While potatoes are still hot, add butter, salt, and pepper.

SCALLOPED POTATOES   Serves 4-6

- ❖ Preheat oven to 350°F.
- ❖ Grease a large baking dish with margarine.
- ❖ Heat milk until it almost boils.
- ❖ Mix all ingredients together in baking pan.
- ❖ Bake for about one hour, or until potatoes are tender.

Ingredients

4 cups potatoes, sliced
1 cup milk
4 Tbsp margarine
1 cup onions, chopped
2 Tbsp flour
2 cups cheese, shredded
garlic powder to taste
salt and pepper to taste

CANDIED YAMS   Serves 6

- ❖ Preheat oven to 350°F.
- ❖ Peel and slice potatoes into $1/2$-inch thick slices and put them in a large pot and cover with water.
- ❖ Boil potatoes for about 25 minutes or until tender. Drain potatoes.
- ❖ Add all other ingredients and mix well.
- ❖ Transfer mixture to baking pan or dish.
- ❖ Bake for 20-30 minutes.

Ingredients

2 lbs sweet potatoes
$1/2$ cup brown sugar
$1/2$ cup granulated sugar
$1/2$ tsp nutmeg
$1/2$ tsp cinnamon
$1/4$ cup margarine or butter
1 tsp vanilla
2 tsp lemon juice
salt to taste

DRIED BEANS

Dried beans are one of the least expensive foods you can eat. Food packagers have never found a way to separate the pebbles from the beans, so be sure to sort through dried beans carefully to pick them out.

Pork is the best seasoning for beans. How much pork you use depends on how lean the pork is; the fattier the pork, the less you need. I suggest using about $1/4$ pound of pork per pound of beans. If you're using lean pork, you should use more.

DRIED BEANS   Serves 4-6

❖ Soak beans overnight or for at least 8 hours
if possible. Although you can cook dried beans
without soaking them, they will take longer to
cook.

❖ Wash and drain beans.

❖ Add pork to beans.

❖ Cover the pork and beans with water.

❖ Cook, covered, over high heat, bringing the water to a boil.

❖ After the water comes to a full boil, simmer the beans for about 1 hour
if they were soaked and at least 2 hours if they weren't. Stir beans occasionally to keep them from being scorched on the bottom of the pot. The beans
will be tender when they're done.

❖ Make sure beans are covered with water while they are cooking by
adding more water if necessary.

Ingredients

1 lb dried beans
$^1/_4$ lb pork

BAKED BEANS   Serves 8

Most people make baked beans by buying
them in a can and adding all kinds of stuff
such as onions, green peppers, brown sugar,
bacon, ketchup, and mustard. Canned baked
beans are convenient, but people usually
overseason them. Homemade baked beans are
cheaper and better.

❖ Soak beans overnight.

❖ Preheat oven to 350°F.

❖ Add beans to boiling water and cook on
stovetop for about $1^1/_2$ hours or until tender.

Ingredients

2 lbs great northern beans or
  navy white beans
1 15-oz can tomato sauce
$^1/_2$ cup brown sugar
1 cup onion, chopped
3 Tbsp margarine
4 strips bacon
$^1/_2$ cup molasses
2 Tbsp mustard
salt and pepper to taste

41

❖ Drain beans.

❖ Fry the bacon until it's crisp.

❖ Combine beans, tomato sauce, brown sugar, margarine, mustard, molasses, bacon, and bacon drippings in a large bowl and mix well.

❖ Transfer ingredients to baking dish.

❖ Bake for 30 minutes.

Serving suggestion: Baked beans are good hot or cold. Some people like to add chopped hot dogs, sausage, bologna, ham, or other meat to this recipe. If you want to add anything, add it before baking.

NO-PORK BAKED BEANS   Serves 8

Many people cannot eat pork for religious or medical reasons. This recipe, which uses no pork, has the same great taste of baked beans cooked with pork.

Ingredients

2 lbs great northern beans

2 cups onion, chopped

2 8-oz cans tomato puree

2 Tbsp margarine

1 cup ketchup

1 cup brown sugar

1 cup molasses

1 tsp salt

$1/2$ tsp pepper

❖ If you are using dried beans, soak them overnight.

❖ Preheat oven to 350°F.

❖ Boil beans in a large pot for $1 1/2$ hours or until they are tender.

❖ When the beans are done, drain excess water from pot.

❖ Put onions and margarine in a small frying pan and fry until brown.

❖ Add remaining ingredients to beans and mix well.

❖ Transfer ingredients to baking pan or dish.

❖ Bake for 30 minutes.

BEAN SOUP   Serves 4

My recipe for bean soup calls for one pound of dried beans. You can use a pound of one type of bean or you can mix all different kinds of beans together.

❖ Soak beans overnight.
❖ Fry bacon strips to a crisp. Do not drain!
❖ Combine ingredients—including bacon drippings—in a large pot and cover with water.
❖ Cook over high heat on stovetop.
❖ After water comes to a full boil, reduce heat and simmer beans for about $1^{1}/_{2}$ hours or until tender.

Serving suggestion: Serve with bread or crackers.

Ingredients

1 lb dried beans
4 strips bacon and drippings
1 medium onion, chopped
1 Tbsp vinegar
1 Tbsp sugar
salt and pepper to taste

KIDNEY BEANS AND RICE   Serves 10

❖ Soak beans overnight.
❖ Boil beans for about $1^{1}/_{2}$ hours or until soft.
❖ Drain excess water, leaving just enough to cover the beans.
❖ Cut sausage into bite-size pieces and fry with onions until onions are brown. Do not drain.
❖ Add sausage, sausage drippings, onions, and other ingredients to beans and simmer for 15 minutes.

Ingredients

2 lbs kidney beans
$^{1}/_{2}$ lb link pork sausage
3 cups cooked rice
1 cup onion, chopped
$^{1}/_{2}$ tsp garlic powder
1 cup ketchup
1 Tbsp chili powder
1 Tbsp sugar
salt and pepper to taste

"To be a great

cook you have to

experiment."

GRAVIES

GRAVIES

*A*nyone who has to live off a limited budget should know how to make gravy. Once you get the hang of it, gravy is very easy to make.

All meat drippings (or grease) or broth (which is the water that meats are boiled in) can be turned into gravy. The secret to learning how to make gravy is trial and error.

If your gravy is too thick, add more milk or water, and if it's too thin, add more flour.

CREAM GRAVY

The meat drippings from a roast, hamburgers, bacon, etc. can be used to make cream gravy.

❖ Add flour to drippings, stirring until the mixture is brown.
❖ Add milk (or milk and water).
❖ Stir this mixture as you scrape the bottom of the pan to be sure that everything is thoroughly mixed.
❖ Add salt and pepper to taste.
Serving suggestion: Get yourself some biscuits and start sopping.

Ingredients

2 Tbsp flour
2 cups milk (you can also use
    1 cup milk and 1 cup water)
salt and pepper to taste
meat drippings

BROTH GRAVY

If you boil a roast, chicken, turkey, or any other kind of meat, you will have broth left over. Making gravy from broth is a little different from making gravy in a frying pan.

Ingredients

4 Tbsp flour
1 cup milk
1 qt meat broth
salt and pepper to taste

❖ Combine milk and flour in a covered container and shake well to mix.
❖ Stir flour and milk into broth.
❖ Cook over medium heat until the gravy comes to a full boil.
❖ Add salt and pepper to taste.

"Anyone who has to live off a limited budget should know how to make gravy."

"Good old Southern

fried chicken giblets

and brown gravy

is a country boy's

dream . . . "

CHICKEN

CHICKEN

When I was a kid, we occasionally had chicken as a Sunday treat. I remember waiting for those chicken dinners with great anticipation—it was almost unbearable! I could taste the crisp fried chicken with gravy days before it was cooked.

Today, chickens are killed, butchered, and packaged for us. Where I grew up, we raised, killed, plucked, and butchered the chickens we ate for dinner. I think it was worth the trouble. Nowadays, chicken is one of the most popular dishes in America because it is relatively cheap. Of course, it costs a lot more than it did when I was growing up. Back then you could buy a chicken for 25¢ and eggs for 12¢ a dozen. I can remember these prices because my brothers and I used to sneak eggs from the hen house, take them to the country store, and trade them for candy. For two eggs, we could each get an "all-day sucker."

BUYING CHICKEN

The poultry department of a grocery store can be overwhelming. There are lots of different kinds of chicken: fryers, broilers, roasters, whole chickens, and chicken parts.

Broilers and Fryers

These are usually young chickens—nine to 12 weeks old. Their meat is tender and the skin is soft, pliable, and smooth. The breastbone is also flexible. Boilers and fryers weigh anywhere from 1^1/$_2$ to four pounds.

Roasting or Baking Chickens

Roasting and baking chickens are usually three to five months old. They also have tender meat, soft skin, and a smooth texture, but the breastbones of roasting and baking chickens are not as flexible as that of broilers and fryers. These chickens weigh from three to five pounds.

50

Stewing or Boiling Chickens

Stewing and boiling chickens are usually mature hens. They are less tender than roasting hens and must be cooked with lots of moisture. Stewing and boiling chickens are used to make chicken dumplings, chicken salad, chicken soup, and more.

Chicken Parts

You can also buy chicken parts: legs, breasts, backs, wings, and livers. Breast meat tops the list in price; backs are the least expensive. All chicken parts taste good, but some are better for certain recipes than others. For instance, necks and backs are great for soup.

Buying a whole chicken is sometimes cheaper than buying two legs, two thighs, and two breasts. Plus, if you buy a whole chicken, you can use the back, wings, and neck for soup.

If you have a freezer, stock up on chicken when it's on sale and freeze what you don't eat right away, but don't forget it's there! Always take stock of your freezer and refrigerator before you go shopping. You'll be amazed at how much money and time this will save you.

STORING POULTRY

Unless you freeze fresh poultry immediately, it should be used within a day or so. Always check the date on the package when selecting chicken. If you can't find a date, be sure to ask the butcher. My wife sniffs meat before buying it. That tells her a lot. She says, "The nose knows."

Poultry, like all fresh meat, must be stored properly. To store uncooked poultry for one or two days, wrap it loosely in wax paper and place it in the coldest part of the refrigerator.

To freeze poultry, wrap it in moisture-proof, vapor-proof paper or bags and store it in the freezer. This way, the poultry can be stored until you are ready to eat it.

Chicken, like all frozen poultry, should be completely thawed before cooking. The best way to thaw it is to move it from the freezer to the refrigerator overnight. If you forget to put the chicken in the fridge overnight, you can place it in a large pot, and cover it in cold, salted water. This will speed up the thawing process.

Since it is dangerous to keep cooked poultry at room temperature for a long period of time, it should be served as soon as possible. Any leftovers should be refrigerated inmediately.

Since bacteria can breed in the cavity of a chicken, remove the stuffing from a stuffed baked chicken before refrigerating.

While there are hundreds of ways to cook chicken, I will only offer a few of my favorite recipes here.

FRIED CHICKEN

Who doesn't like fried chicken? There are fried chicken fast food restaurants all across the country and more are popping up every day. But beware. Buying fried chicken may cost two or three times as much as buying fresh chicken and frying it yourself.

Vegetable and peanut oils work best for frying chicken. Frying may not be the easiest way to cook chicken, but it is definitely the most popular.

Frying chicken takes patience. There is no quick way to fry chicken unless you happen to own an industrial-size vat of oil.

Electric frying pans work well for frying chicken since the heat is distributed evenly. Old-fashioned black iron skillets also work well.

FRIED CHICKEN   Serves 6-8

Ingredients

3 lbs chicken parts
flour
salt and pepper to taste
cooking oil

There are basically two ways of preparing chicken to be fried. Coating the chicken parts in flour before frying is probably the most popular. Some people dip the parts into a mixture of milk, eggs, and flour. If you just coat the chicken parts in flour, you may have leftover flour which can be used to make gravy.

❖ Pour a small amount of flour and salt and pepper to taste into an empty margarine container or a plastic bag. (Depending upon the size of the bag or container, you can usually coat 2 or 3 pieces of chicken at a time.)

❖ Put the chicken pieces in the container or bag.

❖ Put the lid on the container or tie the bag shut and shake until the chicken is coated with flour.

❖ Repeat this process until all of the chicken is coated. Don't forget to save the leftover flour for gravy!

❖ Heat the skillet over a high flame until the surface of the skillet is hot, and then lower the flame so the chicken can fry slowly.

❖ Add cooking oil to skillet until the pool of oil is about $1/2$-inch deep. Heat oil for a few minutes before you begin frying.

❖ Place chicken parts side-by-side so that each part is touching the bottom of the pan. (Do not layer parts.)

❖ Fry parts until they are brown on the underside and then turn them over.

❖ Make sure the bottom of the pan is covered with oil while you're frying the chicken—add more oil if necessary. It will keep the chicken from sticking and burning.

❖ Once the chicken has been browned on both sides, lower the heat, cover the skillet with a lid, and fry for another 30 minutes.

❖ To be sure the chicken is done, cut open one of the breasts. The meat should be white, not red or pink.

❖ If you want to make gravy for the chicken, see recipe on p. 46. Remember, frying chicken is a slow process: be patient! If you try to speed up the process by cooking over a higher flame you will only burn the outside and the inside will be undercooked.

STEWED CHICKEN

Traditionally, hens that could no longer produce eggs were used for stewing. When I was a kid, if my brother and I were hungry for chicken and dumplings, we would tell our mother, "Mom, that old gray hen is too old to lay eggs. We think she's ready for the stew pot." Sometimes, we were bending the truth. Sometimes my mother would find a cluster of undeveloped eggs when she was cleaning the freshly killed hen. When she confronted us we'd say, "Well, guess we were wrong," but she knew what we were up to.

You probably couldn't find a tough old chicken in the grocery store these days. Farmers usually sell them to processing companies to make soup. However, a stewed chicken may still be the best way to get the most out of your grocery dollar. There are several ways to stew (or pot boil) a chicken.

STEWED CHICKEN   Serves 6-8

Ingredients

3 lbs chicken parts
1 Tbsp salt

❖ Start with a pot big enough to hold the chicken and enough water to cover the meat. Be sure to leave room for the water to boil so you don't end up with a mess all over your stovetop.

❖ At this point, you do not have to add any seasoning other than a tablespoon of salt.

❖ Cook over high heat until the water comes to a full boil, then lower heat until the water reaches a slow boil.

❖ It may take up to an hour (or longer) to fully cook the chicken. You can tell if the chicken is done by sticking it with a fork. If the juice comes out clear—not pink—the chicken is done.

❖ Remove the chicken from the pot. For a crispier taste, you can bake the chicken in the oven at 350°F for about 20 minutes after you have stewed it.

CHICKEN DUMPLINGS   Serves 4

There are several things you can do with the $^1/_2$ gallon or so of broth which is left in the pot after you boil a chicken. You can use the broth to make gravy (p. 47). You can also use leftover broth to make dumplings.

Ingredients

2 cups all-purpose flour
2 eggs, beaten
3 Tbsp vegetable shortening
1 cup milk or buttermilk
salt to taste

❖ Combine ingredients in a large bowl and mix until a dough forms.
❖ Roll out the dough until it is about $^1/_2$-inch thick.
❖ Cut the dough into 2-inch squares.
❖ Drop squares of dough into boiling broth and cook for 15–20 minutes or until they are firm.

Serving suggestion: Serve as side dish with chicken and gravy.

BAKED CHICKEN   Serves 4

Ingredients

❖ Preheat oven to 400°F.
❖ Remove the giblets from the chicken, wash the bird, put it in a baking pan, and put it in the oven.

1 6-lb baking chicken (also called a roasting chicken)

❖ Cook the bird for 15-20 minutes or until it is browned.
❖ Cover the baking pan with a lid or aluminum foil. Reduce the oven temperature to 325°F.
❖ It will take roughly 20 minutes per pound to cook an unstuffed chicken. So, if you have a 6-pound chicken, you'd have to cook it for about 2 hours. However, since no two stoves are exactly alike, you should check your chicken often to make sure that you haven't under- or overcooked it. When the chicken is cooked, the inside meat is white, not pink.

Serving suggestion: Serve with gravy and stuffing. See gravy recipe on p. 46

and turkey stuffing recipe on p. 74. Since the chicken is smaller than a turkey, you should cut the turkey stuffing recipe in half. If you have too much stuffing, make patties and place them in the pan around the chicken to cook.

CHICKEN AND RICE   Serves 6-8

❖ Cover the bottom of a large frying pan with cooking oil.
❖ Fry onion, celery, and green pepper.
❖ Cook until vegetables are tender, stirring occasionally.
❖ Add rice, chicken, and chicken broth.
❖ Season to taste with salt, pepper, and garlic powder.
❖ Cook the mixture for about 10 minutes over low heat, stirring occasionally.

Ingredients

1 cup onion, chopped
1 cup celery, chopped
1 green pepper, chopped
4 cups cooked rice
1 cup or 1 10³/₄-oz can
   chicken broth
4 cups cooked chicken,
   chopped
salt and pepper to taste
garlic powder to taste

OVEN-COOKED   Serves 6-8
CHICKEN WITH TOMATOES

Oven-cooked chicken with tomatoes is one of the easiest family meals to prepare. Use your favorite chicken parts for this recipe.

❖ Preheat oven to 375°F.
❖ Place chicken in baking dish or pan and bake for about 30 minutes or until chicken is brown.
❖ Add onions and tomatoes to chicken.

Ingredients

3 lbs chicken parts
1 cup onion, chopped
1 16-oz can chopped tomato
salt and pepper to taste
garlic powder to taste

❖ Season with salt, pepper, and garlic powder to taste.

❖ Let chicken stew in tomato juice for about 1 hour or until the chicken pieces are white in the center.

Serving suggestion: Serve with spaghetti noodles and bread.

OVEN-COOKED CHICKEN WITH VEGETABLES

Serves 6-8

❖ Preheat oven to 375°F.

❖ Place vegetables in a baking pan.

❖ Place chicken on top of vegetables and place pan in oven.

❖ Bake for about 40 minutes, or until carrots are soft.

❖ Season with salt and pepper to taste.

Serving suggestion: Serve with hot bread and noodles.

Ingredients

2 lbs chicken parts

1 10-oz can chopped tomatoes, undrained

5 medium potatoes, quartered

1 8-oz can green peas or corn

2 large onions, quartered

2 cups carrots, thinly sliced

1 cup water

salt and pepper to taste

CHICKEN AND NOODLES

Serves 6-8

Chicken and noodles is an easy dish to make.

❖ Fill two large pots with water. The first pot, which should contain a gallon of water, is for the chicken. The second pot is for the noodles.

❖ Add chicken and onion to first pot.

❖ Cook for 30-45 minutes, or until chicken is tender.

❖ Put second pot over high heat, cover it, and bring water to a rolling

Ingredients

8-10 assorted chicken parts (breasts, legs, thighs, etc.)

1 cup onion, chopped

4 Tbsp flour

1 pint milk

16 oz egg noodles

butter or margarine to taste

boil. Lower heat so that water stays at a slow boil.

❖ In a mixing bowl, combine milk and flour and mix thoroughly.

❖ Pour this mixture over chicken and onions and cook over high heat until it comes to a full boil, stirring occasionally.

❖ Add salt and pepper to taste.

❖ Cook egg noodles in second pot until they are tender.

❖ Season noodles with butter (or margarine).

Serving suggestion: Serve chicken and gravy over noodles.

BARBECUED CHICKEN   Serves 6-8

Barbecued chicken can be cooked on an outside grill or in your kitchen oven.

SAUCE
Homemade barbecue sauce costs a lot less than the store-bought kind. If everyone likes the barbecue sauce you can take the credit. If not, say nothing.

❖ Preheat oven to 350°F.

❖ Combine ingredients in a bowl and mix thoroughly.

❖ Place chicken parts in baking dish with skin down.

❖ Bake for about 20 minutes. When the chicken is done, it will be white on the inside, not pink.

❖ Combine sauce ingredients in bowl and mix well.

❖ Baste the chicken with the sauce and cook for another 15 minutes.

Ingredients

2 lbs chicken parts

Ingredients for sauc[e]

1 cup ketchup

1 medium onion, chopped

1 Tbsp sugar

$1/2$ tsp salt

$1/2$ tsp pepper

1 Tbsp vinegar

$1/2$ tsp chili powder

1 Tbsp Worcestershire sauce

1 Tbsp mustard

$1/2$ tsp garlic

CHICKEN POT PIE   Serves 4-6

I love chicken just about any way it is cooked. But one of my favorite dishes is chicken pot pie. I pig out every time I am near one. See my recipe on pp.120-121 for pie crusts.

Ingredients

3$\frac{1}{2}$ lbs chicken (you can use a whole chicken or chicken parts)

4 medium potatoes, chopped

4 medium carrots, peeled and chopped

2 stalks celery, chopped

1 15$\frac{1}{2}$-oz can peas, drained

2 medium onions, chopped

2 pie crusts (p. 120-121)

3 Tbsp flour

2 Tbsp margarine

salt and pepper to taste

❖ Put the chicken in a large pot and cover it with water.

❖ Boil chicken until it is tender and the meat is no longer pink. You can make your pie crust while the meat is boiling.

❖ If you are using fresh vegetables you should boil them in a separate pot until tender and drain them. If you are using canned vegetables, drain them.

❖ Remove chicken from pot and save broth.

❖ Bone chicken and cut it into bite-size pieces.

❖ Preheat oven to 350°F.

❖ Grease a deep baking dish or pan. You can use butter, margarine, or vegetable oil.

❖ Line the bottom of the baking dish with pie crust dough.

❖ Add the vegetables and chicken to the baking dish.

❖ Add flour and margarine to broth and mix.

❖ Pour enough broth in the baking dish to cover the chicken and vegetables.

❖ Salt and pepper to taste.

❖ Cover chicken pot pie with pie crust dough.

❖ Crimp edges of dough using a fork and poke holes in the top of the pie.

❖ Bake for about 30 minutes or until crust is light brown.

FRIED CHICKEN GIBLETS AND BROWN GRAVY

Serves 4

Ingredients

1 lb giblets
3 Tbsp cooking oil
2 Tbsp flour
2 cups milk
salt and pepper to taste

Good old Southern fried chicken giblets and brown gravy is a country boy's dream, and it is easy to make.

❖ Put several tablespoons of flour in a plastic bag or covered container.

❖ Put giblets in bag or container and shake until giblets are evenly coated.

❖ Pour cooking oil into a large frying pan, covering the bottom of the pan.

❖ After the oil is heated, add giblets.

❖ Fry giblets over medium flame, turning them several times.

❖ To check if the giblets are done, cut one in half. The meat should be white, not pink or red.

❖ Remove giblets from pan. The pan should have enough oil to make gravy. If bottom of pan is not covered with oil, add more.

❖ Add flour to oil and stir until brown.

❖ Add milk and stir, scraping bottom of pan until gravy comes to a full boil. If gravy is too thick, add a little water. If it is too thin, add more flour. Serving suggestion: Serve with biscuits or rice.

QUICK AND EASY BAKED CHICKEN PARTS

Serves 4-6

Ingredients

3 lbs chicken parts
1 8-oz can chicken broth, or
    cream of celery soup, or
    mushroom soup
salt and pepper to taste
garlic powder to taste

This is a very simple, very tasty dish.

❖ Preheat oven to 350°F.

❖ Place chicken parts in a baking dish or pan.

❖ Bake, uncovered, for 15 minutes.

❖ Turn chicken over and cook, uncovered, for

another 15 minutes.

❖ If you are using soup instead of broth, follow the directions on the label, adding the appropriate amount of water. Pour broth or soup over chicken.

❖ Cover with lid or aluminum foil and bake for 30-40 minutes or until chicken is done.

CHICKEN SOUP   Serves 4

You don't have to be sick to enjoy chicken soup. Chicken soup is inexpensive because you can use the least expensive chicken parts, such as backs and necks.

❖ Put chicken and vegetables in a large pot and cover with water.

❖ Cook at a slow boil for about 1 hour or until chicken is tender and the meat is no longer pink in the middle.

❖ Remove chicken and bone it. Cut meat into bite-size pieces and return to pot.

❖ Add seasonings to pot and cook until vegetables are tender.

Serving suggestion: Serve with crackers or bread.

Ingredients

1 lb chicken parts

1 cup onion, chopped

2 cups potatoes, chopped

1 cup carrots, peeled and chopped

1 18-oz can peas, undrained

4 stalks celery, chopped

8 oz chopped tomatoes, ketchup, tomato paste, or tomato juice

salt and pepper to taste

garlic powder to taste

CHICKEN NOODLE SOUP   Serves 4

Chicken noodle soup is very similar to regular chicken soup, except that you add noodles (of course!) and you use fewer vegetables.

❖ Combine ingredients—except noodles—in a large pot and cover with water.

❖ Cook at a slow boil for about 1 hour.

❖ Remove chicken and bone it.

❖ Cut meat into bite-size pieces and return to pot.

❖ Add egg noodles to pot.

❖ Cook for another 15 minutes, or until noodles are tender.

❖ Add seasoning.

Ingredients

1 lb chicken parts

1 cup carrots, chopped

1 cup celery, chopped

1 cup onion, chopped

salt and pepper to taste

garlic powder to taste

2 cups egg noodles

TURKEY

TURKEY

Years ago, only rich folks ate turkey and even then usually only at Thanksgiving or Christmas. These days, turkey is one of the best buys at the meat counter. Unfortunately, many inexperienced cooks are afraid to try to cook these big birds, which is understandable considering how much money you'd waste if you ruined one. My easy, step-by-step directions will have you serving tasty turkey in no time.

HOW TO BUY A TURKEY

Usually, the bigger the turkey, the less it costs per pound. Turkeys come in a whole range of sizes. They can be purchased whole, which is the traditional way to cook a turkey, or in parts, which are great for small families or for people who want a certain kind of meat, such as breast meat, which is mostly white.

There are even more choices: Do you want to buy a fresh turkey or a frozen one? Do you want one that's prestuffed? (By the way, I don't recommend prestuffed turkeys.) To be sure that you are getting exactly what you want, read the label on the turkey carefully. If you are confused and need help, don't hesitate to ask the butcher.

How can you be sure you're buying a tender turkey? The age category on the label is the key. The younger the turkey, the more tender and mild flavored it will be. Young turkeys are usually four to six months old. Roaster turkeys are under 16 weeks old. Designating the turkey's sex—hen or tom—on the label is optional and is an indication of size rather than tenderness.

TURKEY PARTS

Necks

Necks are probably the least expensive turkey part. They are generally used for soup.

Wings

Wings are also inexpensive and can be used in several ways. Wings can be fried, boiled, or baked and served with dumplings.

Legs

Legs are slightly more expensive than necks and wings and are usually cooked the way wings are cooked. Legs have more meat on them than wings do.

Breasts

Breasts are the most expensive turkey part, but they may also be the best buy since you're paying for more meat and less bone than you are with some of the other parts.

FRESH VS. FROZEN TURKEYS

You also have to decide whether to buy a fresh or a frozen turkey. If you are one of those people who likes to shop ahead, then a frozen turkey is your best bet. Look for one that is frozen solid as a rock. A whole frozen turkey—stuffed or unstuffed—can be safely stored in a freezer for up to a year. You don't need to rewrap the turkey unless the packaging it came in has been punctured or torn.

You can save money by buying a large turkey when it's on sale. After you have eaten your fill, the rest can be sliced, diced, and frozen for later meals. When you have removed the meat, the bones can be used to make a great pot of soup.

HOW TO COOK A TURKEY

Some of the stories I have heard about how to cook a turkey are truly comical. There was the lady who stuffed a turkey with popcorn and wanted to know if the turkey would be done when the popcorn popped. Others have cooked turkeys without removing the gizzard, liver, and neck (which are packed in a paper bag inside the turkey).

One common problem is overcooking the bird. Many cooks overcook turkey for fear of not cooking it enough. It is important to cook the turkey until all the red meat turns white and gray (depending upon whether it's white or dark meat), but if you overcook this bird, it will be dry and tasteless. You will also have wasted a lot of meat since the longer you cook a turkey, the more it shrinks.

COOKING A STUFFED TURKEY

You will get better results if you cook the stuffing separately. An unstuffed turkey will cook faster and more evenly, with less shrinkage. It will also keep better longer when refrigerated. Plus, cooking a turkey with its stuffing often encourages cooks to overcook the bird in an effort to make sure the stuffing is done.

MY EASY WAY TO ROAST A TURKEY

❖ Preheat oven to 400°F.

❖ Place the turkey on its back in a roaster pan or in any oven-safe pan that is large enough to hold the turkey. Add about $1/2$ inch of water to pan to keep the bird from scorching.

❖ I do not recommend seasoning or basting the turkey before cooking. Think about it: all you're seasoning when you do this is the skin, which is seldom eaten anyway. Most of the seasoning will probably just end up dripping down into the stock at the bottom of the pan, overseasoning and ruining the stock, which many turkey lovers consider the best part of the bird.

❖ Save the neck, gizzard, heart, and liver for later.

❖ Bake the turkey for about 20 minutes, or until the skin is brown. Browning at a high temperature seals in the juices.

❖ Lower the oven temperature to 325°F.

❖ Cover the turkey loosely with tinfoil. This will prevent overcooking and burning.

❖ I don't follow the timetable on the turkey label anymore. Every time I followed this label, I overcooked my turkey. Since each oven has its peculiarities, cooking times vary. Naturally, the bigger the bird, the longer it will take to cook. Also, it can take as much as an hour longer to cook a stuffed turkey than it would to cook the same turkey unstuffed. Usually, an unstuffed turkey weighing more than 16 pounds will take about $3^1/_2$-$4^1/_2$ hours (or about 20 minutes per pound) to cook at 325°F. If stuffed, that same bird could take $4^1/_2$-5 hours to cook.

The following table can be used as a rough guideline for cooking an unstuffed turkey.

Timetable for Roasting Fresh or Thawed Turkey and Turkey Parts	
Weight	**Cooking Times**
2-$3^1/_2$ lbs (drumsticks, quarters, thighs)	2-$3^1/_2$ hrs
4-6 lbs (breasts)	$1^1/_2$-$2^1/_4$ hrs
6-8 lbs	$2^1/_4$-$3^1/_4$ hrs
8-12 lbs	3-4 hrs
12-16 lbs	$3^1/_2$-$4^1/_2$ hrs
16-20 lbs	4-5 hrs
20-24 lbs	$4^1/_2$-$5^1/_2$ hrs
24-28 lbs	5-$6^1/_2$ hrs

A WORD OF CAUTION

You should never start roasting a stuffed turkey one day and finish roasting it the next. Interrupted cooking increases the possibility of bacterial growth.

It seems every holiday season brings publicity about a new way of cooking turkey, promising excellent results. One that has been publicized recently is long cooking at a very low temperature (250°F). This method is not recommended. At this low temperature, the turkey (and stuffing) might take more than four hours to reach a high enough temperature to destroy bacteria. The turkey would not be safe to eat. Besides, during prolonged cooking the turkey would become dry and tasteless.

TESTING FOR DONENESS

The most reliable method for detecting when your turkey is thoroughly cooked is to use a meat thermometer. A whole turkey is done when the temperature reaches 180°-185°F in the inner thigh. Dark meat turkey pieces are done at 180°-185°F and white meat turkey pieces at 170°F. Your stuffing temperature should reach at least 165°F. To check the stuffing's temperature, just remove the turkey from the oven and insert the thermometer (through the body cavity) into the thickest part of the stuffing. Leave it in for five minutes. The stuffing temperature will rise a few degrees after the turkey is removed from the oven.

There are several other ways to test if the bird is done. Press the fleshy part of the thigh with your fingers. If the meat feels soft, or if the leg moves up and down easily and the hip joint moves easily, or breaks, the turkey is done.

You can also test for doneness by inserting a fork into the thickest area of the inner thigh. If the juices run clear, not pink, the turkey is done.

If you press the skin and it feels hollow between the skin and the meat, the turkey is not only done, it is overcooked and you have dried the sucker out!

While it is important to be sure that the bird is cooked, it is also important not to overcook it. Overcooking wastes time and money. Remember, if the turkey is undercooked you can cook it more, but if it is overcooked, you are stuck with it.

As soon as your turkey is completely cooked, you should remove all the stuffing from the cavities. Harmful bacteria are more likely to grow in the stuffing if it sits in the bird after cooking.

OTHER COOKING METHODS

Rotisserie Cooking

Whole, unstuffed turkeys can be cooked on a rotisserie which turns the meat slowly on a rotary spit over direct heat. Since rotisseries vary greatly, follow the directions that come with the equipment.

Before turning the turkey on the spit, be sure to balance and mount the bird correctly. See that the turkey does not slip as the spit turns.

To mount a whole turkey on a rotisserie spit, attach the neck skin with a skewer to the back of the body. Tie or skewer the wings close to the body. Insert the spit through the length of the body and tighten the holding prongs. Tie the tail and drumsticks firmly to the rod. If properly balanced, the turkey should rotate evenly when the spit is turned.

Timetable for Cooking Turkey on a Rotisserie	
Weight	**Cooking Time**
6-8 lbs	3-3$\frac{1}{2}$ hrs
8-10 lbs	3$\frac{1}{2}$-4 hrs
10-12 lbs	4-5 hrs

Oven Cooking Bags

Preparing a turkey in an oven cooking bag is a moist-heat cooking method that produces a juicy, tender bird.

❖ Preheat oven to 350°F.

❖ Sprinkle flour into the bag to prevent it from bursting.

❖ Place celery and onion in the bottom of the bag to help prevent the turkey from sticking to the bag. Of course, celery and onions also add flavor.

Ingredients

turkey
1 Tbsp flour
1 stalk celery, sliced
1 onion, sliced

❖ Place the turkey in the bag, on top of the vegetables.

❖ Close the bag with the enclosed tie, and cut 6 half-inch slits in the top of the bag to let steam escape.

❖ Insert a meat thermometer through one of the slits.

❖ Set the bagged turkey in a baking dish and put it in the oven.

❖ When the turkey reaches 180°-185°F, it is done.

❖ Cut the top of the bag down the center. Loosen the bag from the turkey so that the bag is not touching the bird and carefully move the turkey to a serving platter.

Use the following chart to determine the cooking time for fresh or thawed turkey cooked in an oven cooking bag.

Timetable for Cooking Turkey in an Oven Cooking Bag		
Weight	Unstuffed	Stuffed
8-12 lbs	$1^3/_4$-$2^1/_4$ hrs	$2^1/_4$-$2^3/_4$ hrs
12-16 lbs	$2^1/_4$-$2^3/_4$ hrs	$2^3/_4$-$3^1/_4$ hrs
16-20 lbs	$2^3/_4$-$3^1/_4$ hrs	$3^1/_4$-$4^1/_4$ hrs

Don't use an ordinary brown bag for roasting because it may not be sanitary. Also, the glue and ink used on brown bags have not been approved for use as cooking material, and may give off nasty fumes. Finally, as the turkey cooks, the juices may saturate the bag, causing it to break during cooking.

Boiling a Turkey

Boiling a turkey may be easier than roasting, but I don't think it's as tasty. Most old-time cooks boiled turkey, even if it was tender enough to roast. Boiling does produce a moist bird with less shrinkage.

❖ Preheat the oven to 350°F.

❖ Place the turkey in a large pot.

❖ Fill the pot with water so that half of the bird is covered.

❖ Cook on stovetop over high heat until the water comes to a full boil and then cut the flame back until the water stays at a slow boil.

❖ To test whether the bird is ready for browning, stick a pronged fork into the thickest part of the breast. If the juice comes out clear—not pink—the turkey is ready to be taken out of the broth and should be placed in a roasting pan to be browned.

❖ Brown the bird for about 20 minutes or until it is a light golden brown.

❖ The broth left in the boiling pot can be used to make gravy (see p. 47).

Microwave Cooking

When microwaving a turkey, check the owner's manual for the size bird that will fit in your oven, and for the cooking time and power level to use. Using an oven cooking bag ensures the most even cooking. Just make sure that you are using a microwave-safe oven cooking bag.

Some microwave ovens do not cook food evenly and "cold spots" develop, especially when cooking dense food like a stuffed turkey. Since some sections of the turkey will be done before others are thoroughly cooked, microwaving a stuffed turkey is not recommended.

Outdoor Cooking

Turkey parts can be cooked on a barbecue grill, and a whole turkey or turkey parts can be cooked in a kettle grill. Charcoal makes a hot fire.

Line the grill with heavy-duty aluminun foil. This will help the meat cook evenly. It will also makes the grill easier to clean. Stack the coals in a pyramid and follow the directions on the lighter fluid bottle. Once the coals are white-hot, spread them to form an even layer.

When using a barbecue grill, be sure the holding racks are six to eight inches from the embers for an even heat without too much intensity. Small turkey quarter roasts are excellent for this method of cooking. Young fryer-roaster turkeys weighing six to eight pounds can be cut into individual servings before barbecuing. The turkey pieces will take at least one hour to cook, depending on their size and thickness. Turn them occasionally while they cook. If they start to char or burn, raise the grill farther from the heat.

When using a covered grill, arrange charcoal on both sides of the fire bowl with a drip pan in the center of the coals. Place the whole turkey on a rack over the drip pan and cover the grill. Add a few coals to the fire each hour. To give the turkey a hickory-smoked flavor, sprinkle one half cup water-soaked hickory chips or flakes over the coals during the last 30 minutes of cooking. The more hickory chips or flakes, the stronger the flavor.

You should allow 15-18 minutes per pound for an unstuffed turkey to cook on a covered grill. For a stuffed turkey, allow 18-24 minutes per pound.

HOW TO STORE LEFTOVER TURKEY, STUFFING, AND GRAVY

So far, so good. You bought the kind of turkey you wanted because you read the label. You thawed it properly and cooked it according to the directions. Now, what do you do with the leftovers?

Handling cooked turkey incorrectly can result in food poisoning. As soon as you take the turkey out of the oven, a countdown begins. From that time, you have about two hours to serve the turkey and refrigerate or freeze the leftovers, including the stuffing and gravy. Why only two hours? Because the bacteria that cause food poisoning can multiply dangerously on food left at room temperature for longer than that.

Take the stuffing out of the turkey as soon as you remove the bird from the oven. Extra stuffing can be kept hot in the oven at 200°F while you eat, or you can refrigerate it.

How you store the leftovers is also important in preventing bacterial growth. Large quantities should be divided into smaller portions and stored in several small or shallow, covered containers. This is because food in small amounts will cool more quickly, stopping bacterial growth.

Leftover turkey will keep in the refrigerator for three to four days. Stuffing and gravy should be used within one to two days. Bring leftover gravy to a rolling boil before serving. For longer storage, wrap leftovers in freezer paper or heavy-duty aluminum foil and freeze them. Proper wrapping will prevent "freezer burn," those white, dried-out patches on the surface of food that make it tough and tasteless. Don't forget to date your packages and use the oldest ones first. Frozen turkey, stuffing, and gravy should be used within one month.

TURKEY STUFFING

I never stuff turkey, but many people do. If you choose to stuff your turkey, the following may be something you should consider. It may seem like a good idea to save time by stuffing your turkey in advance, but that's inviting trouble, because harmful bacteria can multiply in the stuffing and cause food poisoning. Turkeys should be stuffed only at the last minute. Dry stuffing ingredients may be prepared the day before, tightly covered, and left at room temperature. The perishables (butter or margarine, mushrooms, oysters, cooked celery and onions, and broth) should be refrigerated. Combine the ingredients just before stuffing the turkey.

The cavity of the turkey should be stuffed loosely, because stuffing expands as it cooks. Prepare three-fourths cup stuffing for each pound of ready-to-cook turkey. Extra stuffing may be baked separately.

To keep the stuffing in the turkey, you need to close the neck and body cavities. Fold the neck skin over the back and fasten it with a skewer, trussing pins, clean string, or toothpicks. Twist the wingtips under the back of the turkey, resting them against the neck skin. To close the body cavity, use skewers, or tuck legs under a band of skin at the tail, or into metal "hock-locks," if provided. You can also tie the legs together with clean string.

There are folks who will say, "You can eat all the turkey, just save the stuffing for me." Every good cook would like to think that his or her stuffing is better than and a little different from everyone else's. There are tons of different ways to make stuffing and they're all really pretty simple. Stuffing usually includes a mixture of some of the following: eggs, onions, celery, green pepper, watercress, parsley, garlic, tarragon, sage, sweet potatoes, sauerkraut, olives, giblets, oysters, shrimp, crab meat, bacon, ham, pork sausage, ground beef, nuts. Here is a simple recipe for stuffing to get you started. Then you can do your own thing.

TURKEY STUFFING
THE OLD-FASHIONED
WAY AND MY WAY

Makes enough stuffing for a 10-12 lb turkey

Ingredients

$^1\!/_2$ cup butter or margarine

6 cups bread crumbs

1 cup onion, finely chopped

1 cup celery, finely chopped

giblets, chopped (use the giblets that came with the turkey)

1 tsp ground sage

$^1\!/_2$ tsp garlic powder

salt and pepper to taste

You can use store-bought seasoned bread crumbs for stuffing, but I don't think this is the best way to make good stuffing. I think the way granny made stuffing is the best. You will need day-old bread. Toast it lightly or dry it in the oven before using.

❖ Preheat oven to 375°F.

❖ Boil the giblets and turkey neck until tender. Remove the meat from the stock and save the stock.

❖ Fry the giblets, onions, and celery in a frying pan with a small amount of butter, margarine, or cooking oil for about 10 minutes.

❖ Add all the ingredients to the turkey stock and mix until it is soggy.

❖ Stuff the turkey loosely before cooking it. If you have made too much stuffing, you can make patties out of it and cook them alongside the bird in the oven.

❖ If you choose to cook the stuffing separately, which is the way I prefer, you can use these same ingredients and cook them in a baking pan alongside the bird in the oven. The stuffing should bake for 30 minutes—it should not be dry.

CREAMED TURKEY — Serves 4

Creamed turkey is a good way to use up scraps of turkey meat.

❖ Put turkey, onion, and cooking oil in a large skillet.
❖ Fry over medium heat until turkey is brown.
❖ Add flour. Mix and stir until brown.
❖ Add milk, stirring until contents come to a boil.
❖ Add salt and pepper to taste.
Serving suggestion: Serve over hot biscuits, toast, rice, or noodles.

Ingredients

1 cup cooked turkey, chopped
1 cup onion, chopped
4 Tbsp cooking oil
2 Tbsp flour
1 cup milk
1 cup turkey stock or 1 can cream of chicken soup
salt and pepper to taste

TURKEY SOUP — Serves 18-20

After you have trimmed, picked, and pulled most of the meat from the turkey carcass, it will look like something that should be thrown away—and most people do just that—but don't! The bones and scraps will make a delicious pot of soup.

❖ Break the turkey carcass into pieces. Place carcass, turkey scraps, and skin in a large pot.
❖ Add vegetables.
❖ Season with salt and pepper to taste.
❖ Cover soup ingredients with water.
❖ Boil over low heat on top burner for about 30 minutes or until vegetables are tender.

Ingredients

1 turkey carcass
6-8 potatoes, chopped
4-6 celery stalks, chopped
1 8-oz can green peas
3 cups onions, chopped
2 cups carrots, chopped
salt and pepper to taste

❖ Remove bones and skin from pot and serve.

One day I made a big pot of turkey soup from the bones. A friend dropped in and I asked him if he would like to have some.

He looked worried, but he agreed to have a bowl.

After a couple of spoonfuls, he said, "This stuff is good. When I go home I'm going to look to see if the bones I threw in the dog lot are still there so I can make some."

TURKEY POTATO SOUP   Serves 4

❖ Combine ingredients in a large pot and cover with water.
❖ Boil slowly over low heat for about 30 minutes or until potatoes are tender.

Ingredients
1 cup cooked turkey, chopped
2 cups broth
1 cup milk
2 cups potatoes, diced
$1/2$ cup onions, diced
salt and pepper to taste

TURKEY NECK SOUP   Serves 4

❖ Cut turkey necks into 2 pieces.
❖ Put meat in large pot and cover with water.
❖ Boil for about 30 minutes or until necks are tender.
❖ Add other ingredients. Cook until vegetables are tender.

Ingredients
2 turkey necks
1 small onion, chopped
1 cup potatoes, chopped
garlic powder to taste
salt and pepper to taste

❖ Divide the necks equally among servings so that everyone can nibble the meat off the bones.

TURKEY NOODLE SOUP   Serves 6

❖ Combine all ingredients—except noodles—in a large pot and cover with water.
❖ Boil until carrots are tender.
❖ Add noodles and cook until noodles are soft.
Serving suggestion: Serve with crackers.

Ingredients

2 cups cooked turkey, chopped
1 cup carrots, chopped
1 cup onions, chopped
4 stalks celery, chopped
1 $10^3/_4$-oz can cream of celery
    soup or 1 cup turkey broth
salt and pepper to taste
4 cups uncooked egg noodles

TURKEY NECKS   Serves 4
AND DUMPLINGS

❖ Put the turkey necks in a large pot and add about $1/_2$ gallon water.
❖ Boil the turkey necks for about 1 hour or until tender. You should have about $1/_2$ gallon of broth left. If not, add water to the broth until you have that amount. Do not remove turkey necks.

Ingredients

2 turkey necks, cut in half
2 Tbsp flour
1 cup milk
dumpling dough (see biscuit
    dough recipe on p. 21)
salt and pepper to taste

❖ Combine flour and milk in a covered container. Shake the container to mix well.
❖ Add this mixture to broth.
❖ Use a ball of dough about the size of an egg to make a dumpling. Pat the dough balls until they are about $1/_4$-inch thick and drop them into the broth. Boil dough balls for 20 minutes or until they are firm and smooth.
❖ Add salt and pepper to taste.
❖ You can use the leftover broth to make gravy (see recipe on p. 47).
Serving suggestion: Serve the dumplings as a side dish with turkey.

TURKEY WINGS AND   Serves 2
DUMPLINGS

I use this recipe often and I love it. One wing is
enough for one serving, so it's an easy recipe to
scale.

Ingredients

2 turkey wings
2 Tbsp flour
1 cup milk
dumpling dough (see dough
    recipe on page 21.)

❖ Preheat oven to 350°F.

❖ Place wings in pot. Cover with water and
boil for about 45 minutes or until tender.

❖ Remove wings from broth and place in roasting pan. Bake for about 25
minutes or until the wings are crisp and brown.

❖ Use a ball of dough about the size of an egg for each dumpling. Pat the
dough balls until they are ¼-inch thick and drop them into the broth.

❖ Boil dough balls for about 20 minutes or until they are firm and
smooth. Remove dumplings from broth.

❖ In a small mixing bowl, combine flour and milk and mix well.

❖ Add this mixture to broth to make gravy.

❖ Add salt and pepper to taste.

"These days, turkey is one of the best buys at the meat counter."

TURKEY AND RICE   Serves 6

Turkey-flavored rice is an inexpensive meal and it's easy to make!

❖ Pour cooking oil into large frying pan.
❖ Fry onions, green pepper, and turkey until brown.
❖ Add rice, broth, garlic, salt and pepper.
❖ Simmer for 10 minutes.

Ingredients

2 Tbsp cooking oil
1 cup onion, chopped
1 green pepper, chopped
1 cup cooked turkey, chopped
4 cups cooked rice
2 cups turkey broth or 1 $10^{1}/_{2}$-oz
    can cream of chicken soup
$^{1}/_{4}$ tsp garlic salt or powder
salt and pepper to taste

TURKEY SALAD   Serves 6

❖ Mix turkey, celery, sweet pickle relish, and eggs together, stirring gently so that the eggs don't crumble.
❖ In a separate bowl, combine mayonnaise, lemon juice, salt, and pepper.
❖ Pour this mixture over eggs, turkey, celery, and pickles.
Serving suggestion: Serve cold as a side dish or snack.

Ingredients

3 cups cooked turkey, diced
1 cup celery, chopped
$^{1}/_{4}$ cup sweet pickle relish
2 hard-boiled eggs, diced
$^{1}/_{2}$ cup mayonnaise
1 Tbsp lemon juice
salt and pepper to taste

"...You do not have

to use a lot of

fancy seasonings

and spices to make

a tasty meal."

GROUND BEEF

BUYING AND COOKING GROUND BEEF

*I*f you asked a group of 10-year-olds if they would rather have a T-bone steak or a hamburger, nine out of 10 would choose the hamburger.

I have never understood how hamburger got its name. After all, it's ground beef, not ground ham. Hamburgers were originally devised as a way to make use of beef scraps or beef that was too tough for other uses, or beef that was about to go bad. Cheap ground beef usually contains a lot of fat. Sometimes butchers use food coloring or beef blood to hide the fat, but the truth comes out when the beef is cooked and you end up with a pool of grease twice the size of your burger!

Of course, you do need some fat to prevent the burger from drying out when it's fried. Some shoppers buy inexpensive lean beef and have the butcher grind it. Most butchers don't mind doing this for their customers. Some inexpensive hamburger contains leftover chicken or pork scraps. Inexpensive hamburger may also contain added fillers, such as soybeans, which are made to look like ground beef.

Don't be shy about asking the butcher what he or she uses to make ground beef. If you don't like the answer, choose a good, but cheap, lean beef and have the butcher grind it just for you.

The best time to buy hamburger is when it is on sale. You can stock up while the prices are low and freeze what you won't need right away. Ground beef can be safely frozen for several months. You should never freeze ground beef in a large amount, because it will take forever to thaw. Before freezing, the ground beef should be made into patties and each patty should be individually wrapped. This way, you can cook the beef without thawing it.

You do not need to add cooking oil to your frying pan to cook hamburgers. To keep the meat from sticking to the surface of the pan, sprinkle a little salt in the pan. If you are cooking frozen patties, keep the flame low until they are thawed.

If you are oven baking or broiling frozen hamburgers, cook them at 300°F until they are thawed. Once they have thawed, increase the temperature to 350°F and cook until the center of the patty is gray. Be careful not to overcook. If hamburgers are overcooked, they tend to be dry and tasteless. If you like your hamburgers rare, it is better to start with thawed ground beef.

SEASONING YOUR HAMBURGERS

Many cooks mix fillers with ground beef to make more servings and to make the hamburgers tastier. I remember watching my mother mix bread crumbs with ground beef when I was a child.

"Why are you doing that, Mom?" I asked. "Does it make it taste better?"

"No, not really," she said. "It just makes the ground beef go farther, so we'll have enough to go around." She got no complaints from me. Back then, we seldom had hamburgers, so we were glad when mom splurged on ground beef. Fillers such as bread, rice, corn flakes, corn meal, and potato chips do not really make hamburgers taste better, but they do increase the number of servings you can get from each pound. There are, however, other fillers you can add that will enhance the flavor of your hamburgers. The recipes on the next few pages will show you how.

Most cooks have gotten stuck in a rut when it comes to making hamburgers. They simply fry them and slap them between a bun with a few condiments. There's nothing wrong with this traditional method, but it can get old fast.

FRIED HAMBURGERS   Serves 4

Ingredients

salt
1 lb ground beef
cheese (optional)

❖ Sprinkle a little salt into the frying pan. This will keep the hamburger from sticking to the pan and it will also help draw some of the fat out of the beef. Do not add oil or butter.

❖ Fry over low heat. If the grease is sizzling or spattering, the heat is too high—turn it down!

❖ If you are cooking frozen hamburger patties, you can cook them over very low heat until they are thawed and then turn up the heat a little to fry them.

❖ How long you fry your burgers depends on how you like your meat cooked. If you like your meat medium, fry the patties for about 3-4 minutes per side or until the inside has turned gray. For well-done hamburgers, cook the patties until they are light brown in the center. Rarer hamburgers should be fried over high heat until they are scorched on both sides, but you risk live bacteria if you leave your meat pink in the center.

❖ If you want to make cheeseburgers, you can add a slice of cheese over the burgers after they have been flipped and when they are almost done. Continue to cook the burger until the cheese is melted.

ONION HAMBURGERS   Serves 4-6

Ingredients

1 lb ground beef
1 cup onion, finely chopped
$1/4$ tsp garlic
salt and pepper to taste

❖ Before making patties, thoroughly mix onion, garlic, salt, and pepper into ground beef and make patties from this mixture.

❖ Follow recipe for Fried Hamburgers (see above).

TASTY BURGERS

Serves 4-6

❖ Mix ingredients well and make into patties.

❖ Fry the burgers over medium heat for about 4 minutes per side.

Serving suggestion: You may want to make gravy to serve with Tasty Burgers. See cream gravy recipe on page 46.

Ingredients

1 lb ground beef
1 cup onion, chopped
$1/2$ cup ketchup
$1/4$ tsp garlic powder
1 Tbsp sugar
1 Tbsp chili powder
salt and pepper to taste

POOR MAN'S STRETCH BURGERS

Serves 4-6

❖ Mix all ingredients well and make into patties.

❖ Pour cooking oil into frying pan until bottom of pan is covered.

❖ Fry patties over low heat for about 4 minutes per side or until the inside is gray.

Serving suggestion: Serve with a side dish of vegetables or serve the hamburgers in buns.

Ingredients

1 lb ground beef
1 cup onion, chopped
1 cup potatoes, chopped
2 cups bread crumbs
1 cup ketchup
1 $10^3/4$-oz can cream of
    mushroom or cream of
    celery soup
$1/4$ tsp garlic powder
2 Tbsp cooking oil
salt and pepper to taste

POOR MAN'S HAMBURGERS WITH GRAVY

Serves 4-6

Ingredients

1 lb ground beef

1 cup onion, finely chopped

1 cup water

salt and pepper to taste

❖ Make ground beef into hamburger patties and fry them in open skillet until they are cooked to your preference.

❖ Remove hamburger patties from skillet, but do not throw away the oil which has formed at the bottom of the pan. If the oil does not cover the bottom of the pan, you can add cooking oil or butter until the bottom of the pan is covered.

❖ Add onion to pan. Stir over high heat until brown.

❖ Make cream gravy (p. 46).

Serving suggestion: Serve with hot biscuits.

POOR MAN'S GROUND BEEF WITH CHEESE

Serves 4-6

Ingredients

1 lb ground beef

1 cup onion, chopped

1 Tbsp mustard

1 Tbsp sugar

2 Tbsp Worcestershire sauce

$1/4$ tsp garlic powder

salt and pepper to taste

1 cup cheese, grated

❖ Crumble ground beef into large frying pan.

❖ Add onion, mustard, sugar, Worcestershire sauce, garlic powder, salt, and pepper.

❖ Fry over low heat for 6-7 minutes or until meat is browned, stirring occasionally.

❖ When meat is done, stir in cheese and keep over heat until cheese is melted.

Serving suggestion: Serve with rice or bread.

STOVETOP GROUND BEEF AND BEANS

Serves 6-8

❖ Combine margarine, ground beef, onions, and green peppers in a large skillet.

❖ Fry over medium heat until ground beef is browned.

❖ Add remaining ingredients and cook over low heat for about 10-15 minutes.

NOTE: If you leave out the kidney beans, you can also use this as a recipe for spaghetti sauce.

Ingredients

2 Tbsp margarine

1 lb ground beef

1 cup onion, chopped

1 cup green pepper, chopped

$1/4$ tsp garlic powder

2 Tbsp sugar

1 32-oz can tomatoes, chopped

1 Tbsp chili powder

1 16-oz can kidney beans, drained

CHILI

Serves 8-10

❖ Brown onions and beef in a large skillet over medium heat.

❖ Add remaining ingredients to skillet.

❖ Simmer over low heat for 20 minutes, stirring occasionally.

❖ If chili is too dry, add water.

Serving suggestion: Serve with crackers or chips. Some people like to grate cheddar cheese over their chili and top it with sour cream.

Ingredients

1 lb ground beef

1 cup onion, chopped

2 16-oz cans kidney beans, undrained or 2 lbs cooked pinto beans, drained

1 tsp garlic powder

2 Tbsp Worcestershire sauce

1 tsp black pepper

$1/2$ tsp red pepper

1 tsp salt

4 Tbsp chili powder

1 16-oz can tomatoes, chopped and undrained

MEATLOAF

Meatloaf is an inexpensive dish for a large family. But don't despair if you have a small family; it reheats well and can also be sliced for cold sandwiches. Every cook makes meatloaf a little differently. Some people add mushrooms, others add olives. You can use whatever leftover foods you have on hand as filler for your meatloaf.

If you want to add vegetables, they should either be grated or cooked.

POOR MAN'S MEATLOAF WITH GRAVY   Serves 8-12

❖ Preheat oven to 350°F.

❖ Combine everything—except flour and milk—in a large bowl and mix well.

❖ Transfer ingredients to a baking pan or dish and shape the mixture into a loaf.

❖ Bake for about 45 minutes. If clear juice comes out when you stick the loaf with a fork, the meatloaf is done.

❖ Pour off stock into a large frying pan.

❖ Make stock gravy (p. 47).

Ingredients

2 lbs ground beef

2 eggs, beaten

3 cups bread or cracker crum

1 cup onion, chopped

1 16-oz can tomatoes, chopp

1 cup ketchup

1 16-oz can green peas, lima
    beans, or corn, drained

2 Tbsp sugar

1 tsp salt

$^1/_2$ tsp pepper

2 Tbsp Worcestershire sauce

$^1/_2$ tsp garlic powder

4 Tbsp flour

2 cups milk

CHEESE AND PICKLE MEATLOAF WITH SAUCE

Serves 4-6

❖ Preheat oven to 350°F.
❖ Combine ingredients in a large bowl and mix well.
❖ Transfer mixture to a baking pan or dish and shape it into a loaf.
❖ Cook uncovered for about 30 minutes and then remove from oven.

SAUCE
❖ Combine sauce ingredients in a small bowl and mix well.
❖ Pour sauce over meatloaf and cook meatloaf for another 15 minutes.

Ingredients

1 lb ground beef
2 cups bread crumbs
1 cup onion, chopped
1 egg, beaten
1 cup ketchup
$1/2$ cup sweet pickles, chopped
   or relish
$1/2$ tsp garlic powder
$1/2$-1 cup American cheese,
   grated
1 cup milk
1 Tbsp sugar
salt and pepper to taste

Ingredients for sauce

1 $10^3/4$-oz can tomato soup
1 Tbsp mustard
2 Tbsp brown sugar

"Meatloaf is an inexpensive meal for a large family."

STUFFED PEPPERS WITH GROUND BEEF

Serves 6

❖ Preheat oven to 350°F.

❖ Cut stems off peppers and remove seeds.

❖ In a large mixing bowl, combine all other ingredients to make stuffing.

❖ Pack peppers with stuffing and put them in a baking pan or dish.

❖ Bake for about 45 minutes. Stick peppers with a fork. If the juice comes out clear, the peppers are done.

Ingredients

6 large green peppers
1 lb ground beef
1 cup onion, chopped
2 cups cooked rice
1 cup ketchup
1 8-oz can tomato sauce
$1/4$ tsp garlic powder
1 tsp sugar
1 tsp salt
$1/2$ tsp pepper

THE NEST

Serves 4-6

One day my wife asked, "What on earth are you making?"

"A nest," I said.

She said, "It looks more like a mess."

❖ Preheat oven to 350°F.

❖ Put the ground beef in a greased baking dish. Use your hands to form a well (the "nest") in the middle of the pan.

❖ Boil carrots and celery for 20 minutes and then drain.

❖ Pour everything in the nest and cook for about 30 minutes or until potatoes are soft.

Ingredients

1 lb ground beef
$1/4$ tsp garlic powder
2 small onions, sliced
4 potatoes, sliced
3 carrots, quartered
3 stalks celery, chopped
1 16-oz can green peas, undrained
1 10-oz can chicken broth, or cream of celery, mushroom, or broccoli soup
salt and pepper to taste

BEEF

BEEF

You're probably surprised to find beef recipes in POOR MAN'S COOKBOOK. Other than ground beef, there are very few cuts of beef that are inexpensive. However, there are some cuts that fall into the low end of the price range that can be made into a tasty meal. You can buy chuck roast, chuck steak, round steak, or any other cuts with a lot of fat and bone for reasonable prices. But, you have to be the judge of how much fat and bone is included in the price of a given cut of meat. If a particular cut is half fat and bone, that cut of meat costs twice as much as it should.

There are times when it would be better to pay twice as much and get all lean meat. Watch for sales and take advantage of them. Grocery stores discount beef prices when the meat has been on display a little too long and it has darkened. Aging does not hurt beef like it does pork, poultry, and fish. However, if you buy aged meat, you should cook it that very day. Sometimes, butchers discount beef just before closing time. Other times, marked-down beef is on display all the time. I often ask the butcher if he or she has any meat that is going to be marked down that day. I have gotten good steaks for half price this way.

HOW TO COOK BEEF

There are many ways to cook beef. I will list a few of the more common ways. Old-time cooks used to boil beef to make it more tender before roasting it, but this no longer necessary. Most beef sold in grocery stores is tender enough to be cooked as a roast. Beef, unlike pork and chicken, can be cooked to satisfy a variety of tastes: it can be bloody rare, well done, or anywhere in between.

Rare beef is red throughout. It is usually cooked at a very high temperature for a short period of time. Medium-rare beef is light pink on the inside. Medium beef is barely pink. Medium-well beef is light brown on the inside. Well-done beef is gray throughout.

BOILED BEEF ROAST WITH GRAVY

Serves 6-8

Ingredients

3 lb roast

salt and pepper to taste

❖ Preheat oven to 375°F.

❖ Place roast in a large pot and cover with water. Boil over a low flame until you can stick a fork in the roast and the juices run clear.

❖ Remove roast from pot and place in a baking pan. Brown in oven for about 15 minutes.

❖ Make broth gravy (p. 47).

❖ Add salt and pepper to taste.

OVEN ROAST BEEF

Serves 6-8

Ingredients

3 lb roast beef

1 cup water

salt and pepper to taste

garlic powder to taste

❖ Preheat oven to 175°F.

❖ Place roast in baking pan and pour water into pan to prevent roast from getting too dry.

❖ Sprinkle salt, pepper, and garlic on roast.

❖ Cook, uncovered, for about 20 minutes or until brown.

❖ Raise oven temperature to 350°F.

❖ Cover roast with lid or foil. Cook for another 40 minutes.

❖ Keep an eye on the roast near the end of its cooking time to make sure you don't overcook it. Cut into the roast to check whether it is cooked to your liking. Remember, an overcooked roast is dry and will shrink. After roast is cooked to your satisfaction, remove it from pan.

❖ Put pan on a burner and use the drippings to make cream gravy (p. 46). Don't slice more beef than you need for your meal. The leftover roast will keep better if it is not sliced.

BEEF HASH   Serves 6

Never throw away leftover beef. You can refrigerate beef for another meal. You can reheat it and serve it with gravy, dice it into bite-size pieces and add it to vegetable soup, make sandwiches, or make beef hash.

Ingredients

2 cups beef, chopped
1 cup onion, chopped
4 Tbsp cooking oil
$1/4$ tsp garlic salt or garlic powder
salt and pepper to taste
1 cup water
1 cup milk
3 tbsp flour

❖ Combine beef, onion, oil, and seasonings in frying pan and cook over low flame.

❖ Stir well, and cook until onions are brown.

❖ Combine water, milk, and flour in a covered container. Securely cover container and shake to mix well.

❖ Pour this mixture into frying pan and stir.

❖ Simmer over low flame for 15 minutes.

Serving suggestion: Serve with noodles, rice, or hot biscuits.

BEEF POT ROAST   Serves 6-8
WITH VEGETABLES

Ingredients

3 lb roast
2 large onions, quartered
4 large potatoes, quartered
1 cup carrots, sliced
1 8-oz can peas
1 tsp sugar
$1/4$ tsp garlic salt or powder
salt and pepper to taste

❖ Place roast in large pot on stovetop burner and braise (which means to cook slowly in fat with little moisture in a covered pot) for five minutes on each side. Do not add oil.

❖ Add enough water to cover beef, and simmer for about $1^{1}/_{2}$ hours.

❖ Add vegetables to roast and season with sugar, garlic, salt, and pepper.

❖ Cover pot and slowly boil until carrots are tender.

❖ If you want, you can make broth gravy to serve with the pot roast (p. 47).

94

POOR MAN'S   Serves 4-6
SOUTHERN SOPPING
CORNED BEEF WITH GRAVY

Ingredients

3 Tbsp cooking oil

1 12 oz-can corned beef

1 cup onion, chopped

2 cups milk

1 cup water

$^1/_4$ cup flour

salt and pepper to taste

Making a meal with canned corned beef is a great way to stretch a dollar. This is the best-tasting meal you can get from a can of beef! When I was working in L.A., one of my co-workers unexpectedly dropped by at lunch time. I told him that if he would stay for a few minutes he could eat some corned beef with me. I explained to him how I made it and he said, "I have never heard of it being fixed that way." He also said that he had never cared for corned beef.

"Trust me," I told him. "This will be a treat." He watched with great interest as I prepared our lunch. After we had finished sopping eight biscuits each with the delicious corned beef, he said he had never eaten anything that good before. He named it "Southern Sopping."

❖ Cover bottom of large frying pan with cooking oil.

❖ Crumble beef into pan.

❖ Add onion and fry over low flame, stirring until beef is nice and crisp—the crisper, the better.

❖ Add flour and stir until brown.

❖ Add milk and water. Stir, scraping the bottom of the pan, until the mixture comes to a full boil.

Serving suggestion: Sop and eat with biscuits.

BEEF STEW   Serves 8-10

Beef stew can be made with a less expensive cut
of beef, such as chuck roast, as long as the meat
is mostly lean. Some grocery stores sell chuck
roast labeled as beef stew, but this is not the
most economical way to make beef stew. If
there is fat on the beef, leave it on to season the
stew, but remove the fat after the beef has been
cooked. You can use a small amount of beef,
but the more meat the better. If you don't have
much beef, add chicken or pork.

Ingredients

1-2 lbs lean beef
3 medium onions
1 16-oz can peas
1 16-oz can corn
3 stalks celery, chopped
4 carrots, chopped
8 chopped egg-size potatoes
1 tsp garlic salt or powder
salt and pepper to taste

❖ Cut the beef into bite-size pieces.
❖ If meat is tough, boil it in a large, covered pot for 15–20 minutes before
adding vegetables.
❖ Add vegetables and cover with water.
❖ Cook at a slow boil until vegetables are soft.
❖ Pour off stock into another pan.
❖ Use stock to make broth gravy (p. 47).
Serving suggestion: Serve with bread or crackers.

FRIED STEAK WITH GRAVY   Serves 4

Fried steak with gravy is another way to make
the most of your grocery dollar. Plus, it's a
delicious meal. Often the gravy is as good as the
steak. Frying steak is usually the least expensive
cut of beef you can find, although frying steaks
do vary in price. Look for the least expensive cut that the butcher recom-
mends for frying.

Ingredients

1 lb steak
1 cup flour
cooking oil

❖ Coat steak with flour. Save excess flour for gravy.

❖ Cover bottom of frying pan with cooking oil.

❖ Fry steak over low flame until underside is brown.

❖ Flip and brown other side.

❖ Cook steak for about 20 minutes or until it is gray in the center.

❖ Remove steak from pan.

❖ You should have about 4 Tbsp of oil left in the pan. If not, add more until you have 4 Tbsp.

❖ Use oil to make cream gravy (p. 46).

❖ If you want, you can put the steak back into the pan of gravy and let it simmer for 5 minutes.

Serving suggestion: Serve with hot biscuits.

CHICKEN-FRIED STEAK   Serves 6-8
WITH MILK GRAVY

One way to stretch steak to feed a large family is to prepare chicken-fried steak.

Ingredients

2 lbs lean round steak

cooking oil

1 egg, beaten

$1/2$ cup flour

2 cups milk

1 cup onion, chopped

❖ Cut steak into 2-inch squares.

❖ Cover bottom of large frying pan with cooking oil.

❖ Mix egg, flour, and milk in mixing bowl.

❖ Dip steak into this batter.

❖ Fry steak until underside is brown. Flip steak and fry other side until brown.

❖ Remove steak from pan. You should have about 4 Tbsp of oil left in pan. If not, add more until you have 4 Tbsp.

❖ Add onion, leftover flour, and milk to oil and stir, while scraping bottom of pan, until gravy comes to a full boil.

Serving suggestion: Serve with mashed potatoes and hot biscuits.

SWEET PEPPER STEAK

Serves 6

Sweet pepper steak is a good, wholesome meal. Plus, it is inexpensive when green peppers are in season.

❖ Cut steak into 2-inch squares.
❖ Cut onion into bite-size pieces.
❖ Remove seeds from peppers and cut into 1-inch squares.
❖ Pour cooking oil into a large frying pan and heat over medium flame.
❖ Add steak and cook on both sides to desired doneness.
❖ Add remaining ingredients. Turn up heat and cook for about 3 minutes.
❖ Do not overcook onions and peppers; they should be crisp.
Serving suggestion: Serve with rice.

Ingredients

2 lbs round steak
1 cup onion
4 green peppers
3 Tbsp cooking oil
$1/2$ cup soy sauce
salt and pepper to taste

ITALIAN-STYLE STEAK

Serves 6

❖ Pour oil into large frying pan and heat over a medium flame.
❖ Coat steak with flour and brown on both sides.
❖ Add remaining ingredients and simmer for approximately 30 minutes, stirring often.
Serving suggestion: Serve with spaghetti.

Ingredients

2 lbs round steak, sliced
1 cup onion, chopped
1 cup green bell pepper, chopped
1 cup carrots, thinly sliced
1 16-oz can chopped tomatoe
$1/2$ tsp garlic salt or powder
$1/2$ tsp sage
$1/4$ cup cooking oil
salt and pepper to taste

STEAK AND RICE   Serves 4

❖ Cut steak into bite-size pieces.

❖ Pour oil into large frying pan and fry steak over low flame until it is brown on both sides.

❖ Add remaining ingredients and cook over medium flame for about 20 minutes, stirring often.

Ingredients

1 lb steak

$1/2$ cup onion, chopped

1 $10^3/4$-oz can cream of chicken soup (plus water if soup is condensed)

$1/4$ tsp garlic salt or powder

3 cups cooked rice

4 Tbsp cooking oil

salt and pepper to taste

TEXAS BARBECUE STEAK   Serves 6

❖ Cut steak into 4-inch squares.

❖ Coat steak with flour.

❖ Cover bottom of large frying pan with cooking oil.

❖ Fry steak over low flame until brown on both sides.

❖ Add remaining ingredients and simmer over low flame for about 30 minutes.

Serving suggestion: Serve with hot bread.

Ingredients

2 lbs round steak

1 cup onion, chopped

1 cup green pepper, chopped

1 Tbsp sugar

2 Tbsp chili powder

3 Tbsp cooking oil

$1/4$ tsp red pepper

1 cup ketchup

$1/4$ tsp garlic salt or powder

2 cups water, if needed

"Naturally, I believe my mother was the best cook in the world."

PORK

PORK

*P*ork was the most popular meat in the old days because it could be preserved for a long time. As a kid growing up in the country, I remember that when it came time to butcher the hogs—we usually butchered them after the first frost—my brothers and I were overwhelmed with excitement and anticipation. We could almost smell that tenderloin and liver frying.

After we cleaned and butchered the hogs, we cut them up into parts, and trimmed, salted, and packed them in a rat-proof box for the cold winter months to come. The fat was melted down into lard in a big black iron pot out in the backyard. We removed the skins from the hot oil and saved them to make crackling corn bread. Some of the leaner parts of the hog were ground and made into sausage. Parts of the liver, heart, and kidneys were boiled, ground, and made into liver pudding.

My father sold the hams because that part of the hog brought in the highest price. He used the money he earned to buy beans, coffee, and flour. Today, it's hard to imagine someone buying a hundred pounds of pinto beans at once, but my father did.

Whole hams are generally sold four ways: country salt-cured ham, country smoke-cured ham, country smoked precooked ham, and fresh ham. The country salt-cured ham is the most expensive, but the country smoke-cured ham is the most popular. Fresh hams are usually sold for pit barbecue cooking. Hams are also sold in halves, and boneless.

When buying a ham, don't be shy about asking the butcher for details. Is it a lean ham? If not, which brand name is the leanest? Ask any other questions you have. Reading the label very carefully may help you cook a ham properly and bring out the best taste, but you can also cook ham creatively. I will give you a few suggestions to get you started.

Ham can be made into many dishes. It can be served cold or hot. Ham is also used as a seasoning for all types of vegetables. It is also great served with eggs for breakfast or in brown-bag lunches, you can even serve ham biscuits as a party treat . . . the list goes on and on.

HOW TO BUY PORK PRODUCTS

Hams

For a large family, a whole ham may be the way to go. And remember, by using ham to make casseroles, you can get up to 100 servings from an 18-20 pound ham. Be sure to take into account how many big eaters you have. If you are buying for a small family, a half ham may be the best way to go. Remember the butt end of the ham may cost a little more, but you will find more meat and less bone in this half. If you are pressed for time, you can buy a fully cooked ham, but read the label carefully, because even pre-cooked hams need to be cooked for a while.

Fresh Ham

Fresh hams have no preservatives to keep them from spoiling. Therefore, fresh ham must be kept in the refrigerator until it is cooked. It should be cooked within a day of purchase.

Pork Shoulder

Pork shoulder, sometimes called picnic ham, is confusing to some people. Remember, a ham is the back leg of a hog and the shoulder is the front leg. Smoked cured pork shoulder is sold for much less than ham and sometimes you can hardly tell the difference in taste, but the shoulder has much more fat on it than a ham does.

Pork Chops

Pork chops are popular but they are also pretty expensive. Make sure that you're not paying for a lot of fat and bone when you select your pork chops. Compare the prices for pork chops and boneless pork tenderloin: Even if the boneless tenderloin costs twice as much as chops, the tenderloin may be a better buy, since you're paying for less bone and fat.

Pork Sausage

There are many brands of sausage, none of which taste quite the same. The price may be governed by how much fat it contains and what's been added. Read the label carefully to figure out what's been added to each brand of sausage.

Bacon

Bacon is perhaps best known as something to eat for breakfast, but there are lots of other ways to serve it. It can be used to season dry beans and other vegetables and for frying lean meats.

Leftover bacon grease should be stored in a leak-proof, heat-resistant container and refrigerated for later use. Even if you don't plan to use the grease for seasoning or something else, don't dump it down your sink because it will clog the pipes and a plumber will charge you a whole lot of bacon to get it out.

HOW TO COOK A SMOKED HAM

There are lots of different ways to prepare baked ham. You can fuss over it by using all kinds of seasonings, pouring or rubbing them on. One time, I was trying to think of something different I could do with a ham I was cooking. I opened a cabinet door and there sat a full gallon of apple cider. "That's it," I said under my breath. "I'll pour all of that cider over and around the ham." A friend ate some and said it was the best ham he had ever had.

I think the best way to cook a ham is to boil it first and then bake it. A boiled ham retains moisture better and doesn't shrink as much.

It is very hard to determine when a ham is done. Be careful not to overcook ham. Remember, if you undercook ham, you can always stick it back in the oven, but if you overcook it, there is nothing you can do to fix your mistake. Most hams and pork shoulders have cooking directions printed on their wrappers. These are usually a big help.

Ham, like turkey, has to be cooked slowly due to its thickness.

This is true whether you are boiling or baking it.

❖ If you are boiling a ham, put it in a large pot and cover it with cold water. Bring water to a slow boil. Boil the ham for 20 minutes per pound.

❖ If you are baking the ham, put about 1 inch of water in the baking pan. This will prevent the drippings from burning and will help to keep the ham moist.

❖ Bake the ham at 375°F for about 20 minutes or until it is brown.

❖ After ham is browned, reduce oven temperature to 325°F. Cover with lid or foil to finish cooking. I suggest baking ham 20 minutes per pound. You can also use a meat thermometer. Ham is done when the thermometer registers 140°F.

HOW TO COOK A COUNTRY SALT-CURED HAM

Never cook a salt-cured ham without first trying to get most of the salt out of it. This is done by soaking and changing the water three or four times over a period of 24 hours. If you don't soak it, the ham will be too salty to eat.

The best way to cook a country salt-cured ham is to boil it. After the ham has boiled for 15 minutes or so, change the water and continue to boil it. There are some cooks who will add a cup of vinegar and a cup of brown sugar to the water for seasoning. To test for doneness, place a meat thermometer in the thickest part of the ham, being careful not to hit the bone. When the ham's temperature reaches 140°F, the ham should be done.

HOW TO COOK FRESH PORK HAM OR SHOULDER

It is not necessary to season a fresh ham or shoulder before cooking it. It is better to season the meat right before serving it. Fresh ham can be served for any meal. Leftover ham or shoulder can be sliced and re-heated in a frying pan and served with eggs for breakfast.

Fresh pork ham or shoulder can be baked until it is done, or you can boil and bake it. I prefer boiling it first and then baking it.

❖ Preheat oven to 325°F.
❖ Place the pork ham or shoulder on a meat rack in a baking pan so that you do not burn the bottom of the meat. If you don't have a rack that will fit in the pot, you can use an upside down aluminum pie pan.
❖ Bake for about 2½-3 hours. (If you want to boil and bake the meat, you can boil it for 1½ hours and then bake it for 30-40 minutes at 325°F.) Serving suggestion: Ham goes well with fried apples, applesauce, cooked dried beans, and apple butter.

POOR MAN'S   Serves 6
HAM CASSEROLE

❖ Preheat oven to 350°F.
❖ Combine ingredients in a large baking pan.
❖ Cook for 30 minutes.

Ingredients

2 cups lean, cooked ham, chopped
2½ cups uncooked macaror
2 eggs, beaten
1 cup onion, chopped
1 Tbsp cooking oil
1 cup milk
2 Tbsp flour
.12 oz cottage cheese
4 Tbsp ketchup
1 tsp salt
1 tsp pepper
sprinkle of garlic salt or garli
    powder

HAM, RICE, AND PEAS   Serves 4-6

❖ Preheat oven to 350°F.

❖ Grease a large baking dish.

❖ Combine ingredients in baking dish.

❖ Cook for 30 minutes.

Ingredients

2 cups cooked ham, diced

4 cups cooked rice, drained

1 10-oz can green peas

1 cup cheese, diced

4 hard-boiled eggs, sliced

1 cup onion, chopped

1 cup milk

2 Tbsp flour

$1/2$ tsp salt

$1/4$ tsp pepper

sprinkle of garlic salt or garlic powder

PORK SAUSAGE

Pork sausage, like ground beef, is usually made from the trimming or scraps of the hog. The leaner pork sausage is, the better it is. Store-bought sausages vary widely in taste. The only way to find a sausage that suits your taste is to try several brand names. Good lean sausage will not melt away to grease. As with any other type of pork, sausage should be thoroughly cooked to avoid contracting a disease called trichinosis. Always carefully wash your hands and any utensils that touch raw pork.

Most store-bought sausage is preseasoned, so there is little work to be done when preparing it. Uncooked pork sausage is usually seasoned with some, or all, of the following seasonings: black pepper, red pepper, salt, sage, thyme, ground bay leaves, sweet marjoram, coriander, and summer savory.

Sausage has always been served as a breakfast treat—it is usually served with eggs. However, sausage can also be served as a main dish, in a casserole, in meatballs, in sausage gravy, and in many other ways. Sausage can also be fried or broiled. Fresh sausage should never be left unrefrigerated and should always be used within two or three days of purchase. Sausage can be frozen in links or as patties.

One of the most common ways to cook sausage is to slice the meat into patties and fry them in an open skillet. You do not need to add any oil to the pan; the sausage has enough fat to take care of that. Sausage has to be cooked thoroughly, but overcooking will cause dryness. To avoid this, fry patties over a low flame until they are gray (not red) in the center.

PORK SAUSAGE WITH MILK GRAVY

Serves 4-6

For a sopping good meal, it is hard to beat sausage with milk gravy. Plus, it is so simple to make.

Ingredients

$^1/_2$ lb sausage
3 Tbsp flour
2 cups milk

❖ Crumble sausage into a skillet.
❖ Fry sausage over medium heat until it is brown.
❖ Combine flour and milk in a covered container. Shake well to mix.
❖ Pour this mixture over sausage and stir for a minute, or until it comes to a boil.
Serving suggestion: Serve with hot biscuits.

SAUSAGE WITH RICE

Serves 6

❖ Crumble sausage into a large skillet.
❖ Add onion and fry until sausage is brown.
❖ After sausage is cooked, add remaining ingredients and let simmer in covered skillet for 20 minutes.

Ingredients

$^1/_2$ lb sausage
$^1/_2$ cup onion, chopped
4 cups cooked rice
1 8-oz can cream of celery or
    cream of chicken soup (add
    water to canned soup if the
    label calls for it)
1 cup milk
salt and pepper to taste

PORK SAUSAGE AND MACARONI

Serves 6

❖ Preheat oven to 350°F.

❖ Crumble sausage into a large skillet.

❖ Add onion and fry until sausage is brown.

❖ Place sausage and onion in baking dish.

❖ Add remaining ingredients and mix.

❖ Cook in oven for 30 minutes or until macaroni is soft.

❖ Add water, if needed, to take away dryness.

Ingredients

$^1/_2$ lb sausage

1 cup onion, chopped

3 cups uncooked macaroni

1 16-oz can whole tomatoes, undrained

1 cup water

2 Tbsp sugar

1 10$^3/_4$-oz can cream of celery soup

salt and pepper to taste

SAUSAGE CASSEROLE

Serves 6

❖ Preheat oven to 350°F.

❖ Crumble sausage into a frying pan. Add onions, pepper, celery, and bread crumbs and cook, uncovered, until sausage is brown.

❖ Add remaining ingredients and mix well.

❖ Place in baking pan and cook for 30 minutes.

Ingredients

1 lb sausage

1 cup onion, chopped

1 green pepper, chopped

1 cup celery, chopped

3 cups bread crumbs

2 eggs, beaten

1 cup applesauce

1 16-oz can whole tomatoes, chopped

1 can cream of chicken soup

1 cup cheese, grated

1 cup milk

salt and pepper to taste

109

PORK CHOPS

Nothing makes a country boy happier than Southern fried pork chops with brown gravy and hot biscuits. As with other meats, there are many ways to cook pork chops. Here are recipes for some popular methods.

FRIED PORK CHOPS   Serves 4

Ingredients

4 large pork chops
2-3 Tbsp flour
cooking oil
salt and pepper to taste

❖ Coat pork chops with flour in a bowl. Save the leftover flour for making gravy.
❖ Cover bottom of large frying pan with cooking oil.
❖ Fry chops over low flame, turning occasionally. Cook for about 30 minutes or until the chops are white in the center. Do not overcook by letting the chops become dry like wood chips.
❖ After chops are done, remove from pan.
❖ Make cream gravy (p. 46).
Serving suggestion: Serve with hot biscuits and mashed potatoes.

PORK CHOPS   Serves 6
AND TOMATOES

Ingredients

6 large pork chops
2-3 Tbsp flour
garlic powder to taste
salt and pepper to taste
1 medium onion, chopped
2 16-oz cans chopped
    tomatoes, undrained

❖ Preheat oven to 350°F.
❖ Coat chops with flour and place them in baking pan. Do not layer chops.
❖ Add garlic powder, salt, and pepper to taste.
❖ Cook in oven for 30 minutes, turning chops once to allow them to brown on both sides.
❖ Add onions and tomatoes.
❖ Cook for another 30 minutes.
Serving suggestion: Serve with spaghetti or bread.

PORK CHOPS WITH RICE Serves 4

❖ Coat chops with flour.

❖ Cover bottom of large skillet with cooking oil.

❖ Fry chops in skillet until they are brown on both sides.

❖ If you have more than 4 Tbsp oil left, remove the excess.

❖ Add rice, onions, and soup.

❖ Simmer for 15 minutes, stirring occasionally.

Ingredients

4 pork chops

flour

cooking oil

2 cups cooked rice

1 cup onion, chopped

1 8¾-oz can cream of chicken, celery, or broccoli soup (add water to the soup if the label calls for it)

garlic powder to taste

salt and pepper to taste

BARBECUED PORK CHOPS Serves 6

❖ Preheat oven to 350°F.

❖ Place chops in baking pan and cook for about 20 minutes or until they are brown on both sides.

❖ Mix all other ingredients in a bowl and pour over chops.

❖ Cook for about 1 hour.

Serving suggestion: Serve with spaghetti noodles, rice, or bread.

Ingredients

6 large pork chops

1 cup onion, chopped

1 green pepper, chopped

½ cup ketchup

1 16-oz can tomatoes, undraine

3 Tbsp vinegar

¼ cup sugar (white or brown)

¼ tsp garlic powder

2 Tbsp Worcestershire sauce

pinch of red pepper

salt and pepper

1 Tbsp chili powder

1 Tbsp mustard

SWEET AND SOUR PORK CHOPS

Serves 6

❖ Preheat oven to 350°F.

❖ Place pork chops in baking pan and cook, turning pork chops until both sides are brown.

❖ Add remaining ingredients—except fruit cocktail.

❖ Cook for 20 minutes.

❖ Add fruit cocktail and cook for another 30 minutes.

Serving suggestion: Serve with rice.

Ingredients

6 large pork chops
1 cup onion, chopped
1 green pepper, chopped
1 cup carrots, thinly sliced
3 Tbsp mustard
$\frac{1}{2}$ cup brown sugar
3 Tbsp vinegar
$1\frac{1}{2}$ tsp cinnamon
1 cup water
1 16-oz can fruit cocktail, undrained

PORK ROAST

Serves 6-8

Pork roasts are cut in several ways. Both boneless roasts and rib roasts can be placed in a baking pan and cooked in the oven. You can put all kinds of seasonings on your roast, or you can cook it without any seasonings. I have never been able to taste the difference.

Ingredients

5 lb roast, with bone
salt and pepper to taste
garlic powder to taste
2 cups milk
2 Tbsp flour

❖ Preheat oven to 350°F.

❖ Place roast in a baking pan, with the fattier side up.

❖ Sprinkle roast with salt, pepper, and garlic powder.

❖ Cook for 30 minutes or until brown.

❖ Lower temperature to 325°F.

❖ Cover pan with lid or aluminum foil. Cook for about $1\frac{1}{2}$ hours. The amount of cooking time depends on the size of the roast. When the meat is white, not red, all the way through, it is done. If you have a meat thermometer, you can use it to test for doneness. When the thermometer reads 160°F, the roast is done.

❖ Remove the roast from the pan.

❖ You should have enough drippings in the pan to make gravy. Combine flour and milk in a covered container and shake well.

❖ Pour this mixture into the pan and stir the gravy until it comes to a full boil.

Serving suggestion: Serve with applesauce or baked apples.

BOILED PORK ROAST   Serves 6-8

I prefer to boil pork roast. A boiled roast shrinks less and cooks faster.

Ingredients

4 lb pork roast

❖ Place roast in a large pot, cover roast with water, and cover pot with lid.

❖ Cook over high heat on stovetop burner until water comes to a full boil, then reduce heat.

❖ Cook at a slow boil for about 1 hour, or until meat is tender.

❖ Preheat oven to 325°F.

❖ Remove roast from pot and put it in a baking pan. Save the stock in the pot.

❖ Cook the roast in the oven for 30 minutes.

❖ Make broth gravy (p. 47).

PORK RIBS   Serves 4

Ingredients

3 lbs pork ribs

You should buy pork ribs chopped to serving
size. I usually boil ribs before baking them to
keep them moist; baking pork ribs dries them out too much.

- ❖ Preheat oven to 350°F.
- ❖ Boil ribs in a large pot for 1 hour, or until tender.
- ❖ You can either bake the ribs in the oven or barbecue them. If you want
to make barbecued ribs, use the barbecue sauce recipe on page 58. If you
want to bake the ribs, transfer them to baking pan and bake for another 30
minutes or until the meat is gray in the center of the rib.
- ❖ Remove ribs from pot.
- ❖ Make stock gravy (p. 47).

DESSERTS

DESSERTS

For most of us, no meal is complete without some sort of sweet. Kids would eat nothing but sweets if they were allowed to. I think I'm one of those kids.

SWEET POTATO OR PUMPKIN PUDDING

Serves 8

Pudding is easier to make than pie because you don't have to make a crust. Sweet potato or pumpkin pudding can be served as a dessert or as a vegetable side dish.

❖ Place potatoes or pumpkin in a large pot.
❖ Cover with water and boil until tender.
❖ Drain off all water and mash potatoes or pumpkins with an electric mixer or a hand-held potato masher.
❖ Add remaining ingredients to pot and mix well.
❖ Preheat oven to 350°F.
❖ Transfer ingredients to baking dish.
❖ Bake for 30 minutes.

Ingredients

6 cups sweet potatoes, cooked and peeled or 6 cups pumpkin, cooked and peele
$^1/_2$ cup margarine
1 level tsp salt
1 cup sugar (white or brown)
$^1/_2$ tsp cinnamon
2 Tbsp vanilla
$^1/_2$ tsp nutmeg
1 cup molasses
2 eggs, beaten

"... No meal is complete without some sort of sweet."

SMACK YOUR LIPS   Serves 6-8
RICE PUDDING

❖ Preheat oven to 350°F.

❖ Combine ingredients—except margarine
and nutmeg—in a large mixing bowl and mix
well.

❖ Transfer ingredients to a baking dish.

❖ Cook for 30 minutes.

❖ Stir in margarine while hot.

❖ Sprinkle nutmeg on top.

Serving suggestion: Serve pudding with a dab
of whipped cream on top.

Ingredients

3 cups cooked rice

1 cup sugar

1 tsp salt

4 eggs, beaten

3 cups milk

2 tsp vanilla

$1/2$ cup raisins

4 Tbsp margarine

$1/2$ tsp nutmeg

DOWN-HOME   Serves 6
BREAD PUDDING

Ingredients

❖ Preheat oven to 350°F.

❖ Combine all ingredients—except bread—in
a large bowl and mix well.

❖ Grease baking dish with margarine.

❖ Transfer ingredients to baking dish.

❖ Cut slices of bread into 4 pieces.

❖ Press bread into mixture so that the top of
the baking dish is covered with bread.

❖ Cook, uncovered, for 40 minutes. Bread
pudding should be moist, not dry, when it's done.

8 slices white bread, lightly
    toasted

3 eggs, beaten

$1^{1}/2$ cups sugar

2 Tbsp margarine

3 cups milk

1 Tbsp vanilla

$1/2$ tsp nutmeg

$1/2$ tsp salt

COUNTRY BOY CORN PUDDING

Serves 6

Corn pudding can be served as a dessert or as a vegetable. It is a good down-home dish however you serve it.

❖ Preheat oven to 350°F.
❖ Combine ingredients in a large baking dish and mix well.
❖ Bake for 30-45 minutes.

Ingredients

1 16-oz can creamed corn
3 Tbsp flour
4 Tbsp sugar
1 1/2 cups milk
3 eggs, beaten
1 tsp salt
4 Tbsp margarine, melted

BANANA PUDDING

Serves 8-10

❖ Cover the bottom of a 9" x 12" glass baking dish with wafers.
❖ Cut the bananas into 1/4-inch slices and cover the wafers with a layer of bananas.
❖ Add another layer of wafers.
❖ Add another layer of bananas.
❖ Continue this process until you have used up all of the bananas and vanilla wafers.
❖ Follow directions on box to make pudding.
❖ Add whipped cream to pudding and stir well.
❖ Pour the whipped cream-pudding mixture over the bananas and wafers.
❖ Refrigerate pudding until it is time to serve it.
Serving suggestion: Banana pudding tastes best when it is served the day after you make it.

Ingredients

1 12-oz box vanilla wafers
5 large ripe bananas
1 box instant vanilla pudding
   mix
8 oz whipped cream
3 cups milk

SHAKY PUDDING

Serves 6

Shaky pudding is quick and easy to make. It's also tasty.

❖ Follow the directions on the instant pudding box to make the pudding.

❖ Stir in the fruit cocktail and the shaky pudding is ready to serve.

Ingredients

1 box vanilla instant pudding mix

1 16-oz can fruit cocktail, undrained

POOR MAN'S SWEET BREAD

Serves 6

This recipe was used by our ancestors who couldn't run out to the store to buy 25 different kinds of cookies. Sweet bread is good served hot or cold. It is made much like you make regular bread.

❖ Preheat oven to 350°F.

❖ Combine all ingredients—except margarine or shortening—in a large mixing bowl and mix well.

❖ Add margarine or shortening. Work it into this mixture using a fork.

❖ Add milk and mix until a batter forms.

❖ Transfer batter to a bread pan.

❖ Cook for about 15 to 20 minutes.

Ingredients

2 cups all-purpose flour

1 cup sugar

2 eggs, beaten

$^{1}/_{2}$ tsp nutmeg

2 tsp baking powder

1 tsp cinnamon

$^{1}/_{2}$ tsp soda

1 tsp salt

$^{1}/_{2}$ cup milk

2 tsp vanilla

1 cup margarine or shortening

PUMPKIN CAKE   Serves 6-8

❖ Preheat oven to 350°F.

❖ Mix eggs and sugar in a large mixing bowl.

❖ Add remaining ingredients to bowl with eggs and sugar and mix.

❖ Pour batter into greased cake pan.

❖ Cook for 20-30 minutes. Stick a toothpick into the center of the cake. If it comes out clean, the cake is done.

Ingredients

4 eggs, beaten

2 cups sugar

2 cups canned cooked pumpki

2 cups milk

2 cups all-purpose flour

1 cup margarine or shortening
    melted

2 tsp baking powder

1 tsp cinnamon

1 tsp salt

PIE CRUST   Makes 1 pie crust

Making your own pie crust saves money and gives you a better pie. The best pies do not start with a store-bought crust! Besides, when you buy a ready-made pie crust, you are also paying for the aluminum pan. Go out and buy one or two good metal pie pans—they will last forever! Making your own pie crust is inexpensive because you need only a few ingredients.

Ingredients

$1/2$ cup milk

4 Tbsp vegetable shortening

$1/2$ cup milk

2 Tbsp sugar

1 tsp salt

$1^1/2$ cups all-purpose flour

❖ Heat milk in a large pot on the stovetop.

❖ Add vegetable shortening to milk and stir until the shortening has melted.

❖ Add all other ingredients—except flour—to this mixture and mix well. Remove from heat.

❖ Add flour a little at a time, stirring this mixture with a fork, until it forms a thick dough. To keep dough from sticking to you and everything else, sprinkle flour on everything the dough will touch—the breadboard, the rolling pins, and your hands!

❖ Chill dough in refrigerator for about 30 minutes so that it will be easier to shape and cut.

❖ Using a rolling pin, roll dough to about $1/8$-inch thick.

❖ Wrap the dough around the rolling pin to transfer it to the pie pan.

❖ Using a fork, press the dough to the edge of the pie pan and cut off excess.

❖ If you want to cook the crust before filling it, bake it at 350°F for 5-10 minutes or until the crust is golden brown.

PIE

Whenever I think of pies, I remember one time my brother and I came home from school to a wonderful smell. We were about nine and 10 years old at the time. The closer we got to our house, the more we could smell something sweet. We started walking faster, following the scent around to the back porch. When we first spotted the eight chocolate pies cooling on the back porch, we thought we were dreaming.

We hadn't had a piece of pie for several months. We looked around for our mother, but she was nowhere in sight. Without saying a word to each other we knew what we had to do. We each grabbed a pie and took off for the barn. We knew we'd get our tails whipped if we were caught, but the pies would have been worth the pain. We ate every last crumb!

Thirty minutes later we were both dog sick. When our mother told us that two pies were missing, we suggested that some hound dogs may have gotten them. She believed us until we didn't want any chocolate pie for dessert that night. "I think I know which hounds those were," our mother said.

APPLE PIE   Serves 6

Ingredients

6 small apples or 4 large apples,
   peeled and diced
1 cup sugar (add more if you're
   using tart apples)
3 Tbsp flour
1 tsp cinnamon
1 tsp nutmeg
1 tsp vanilla
3 Tbsp margarine, melted
2 pie crusts (p. 120-121)

Making apple pie is a great way to use up apples that are close to going bad.

Most people buy apples by their looks. They think if it's shiny and pretty it must be good, but this isn't true. Some apples are better for cooking and others are better for eating raw. So, when you're shopping for apples, don't decide which ones to buy based on the way they look, buy the ones that are the least expensive. If you don't know which apples are best for the recipe you are using, ask someone in the produce
department to help you. Remember, Red Delicious, Golden Delicious, and Granny Smith apples are not the only apples that taste good.

❖ Preheat oven to 350°F.
❖ In a large mixing bowl, add diced apples to other ingredients and stir well.
❖ Line pie dish with pie crust and cut off excess dough.
❖ Fill the pie dish with diced apple mixture.
❖ Cover pie with pie crust. Crimp crust to edge of pie dish using a fork. Cut off excess dough.
❖ Brush milk over top crust and sprinkle it with sugar.
❖ Poke the crust with a fork in several places to allow steam to escape.
❖ Cook for 45 minutes or until crust is golden brown. Stick a toothpick into the center of the pie to check if it's done. If the toothpick goes through the apples easily, the pie is done.

INDEX

SUBJECT INDEX

NOTES

NOTES